GOOD AFTERNOON GENTLEMEN,
THE NAME'S
BILL GARDNER

GOOD AFTERNOON GENTLEMEN, THE NAME'S BILL GARDNER

BILL GARDNER
WITH CASS PENNANT

JOHN BLAKE

Published by John Blake Publishing Ltd,
3 Bramber Court, 2 Bramber Road,
London W14 9PB, England

www.johnblakepublishing.co.uk

First published in paperback in 2006

ISBN 978 1 84454 261 1

British Library Cataloguing-in-Publication Data:

A catalogue record for this book is available from the British Library.

Design by www.envydesign.co.uk

Printed in the UK by CPI Bookmarque, Croydon, CR0 4TD

7 9 10 8 6

Papers used by John Blake Publishing are natural, recyclable products made
from wood grown in sustainable forests. The manufacturing processes conform
to the environmental regulations of the country of origin.

I would like to dedicate this book to David Gray, a Spurs fan and a good friend, who died in 2004 after losing a lengthy battle against cancer. In spite of his own terminal illness, he was always helping others and was an inspiration. For me he was the bravest man I've ever known.

Contents

Prologue

By Ian 'Butch' Stuttard

Seen from a distance, a gathering of football supporters looks like a gathering of football supporters, regardless of what team they follow or what colours, shirts or other identifying marks are on display. But a firm looks like a firm. The violent hooligan element associated with any football club is different from its main body of fans. This firm has an edge and a purpose that is absent from those turning up simply to watch a game of football and cheer their team on. Within a group like this, some characters stand out. Not necessarily because of their physique or demeanour, but because they are the leaders, the strategists, the ones with initiative, those to whom others turn when things go wrong. Such a man is Bill Gardner. His loyalty is to West Ham and his reputation is well respected among the fans who travel regularly to away matches.

GOOD AFTERNOON, GENTLEMEN, THE NAME'S BILL GARDNER

I first came to know Bill Gardner through the ICF (InterCity Firm) in the 1984/85 season, when I was making a documentary film for Thames TV called *Hooligan*. By then, Bill Gardner had been around for some time. To some of the fans on the terraces, and certainly to the hardcore ICF, he was renowned. His experience boosted the ICF's young turks: Cass Pennant, Andy Swallow and their cohorts. They showed Gardner due respect, just as the ICF's junior branch (known as the Under 5s) deferred to them. Although Gardner and his colleagues remained independent and seemed to be semi-retired from hooligan activity by that stage, whenever a meaty confrontation loomed in the fixture list, anticipation would grow as the word went round that Gardner would be along to swell the ranks of the ICF.

Bill is a big man and solid, but as he readily admits he has never been fleet of foot. Yet he has always known when to stand, hold fast and face what's coming at him. 'Find the high ground, or somewhere where you've got your back to the door, so you can see what's coming in front of you. Never be caught in the middle where people can get around you.'

I witnessed a graphic example of Gardner in action after a mid-table First Division match when West Ham visited Nottingham Forest during the 1984/85 season. Although the travelling ICF numbered only about 15, the party included Gardner, Big Ted and Andy Swallow. This was a much-travelled and battle-hardened group. At half-time inside the ground the Nottingham boys stepped up to the ICF and fighting erupted in the toilets and at the pie stall at the back of the stand. I began filming the encounter with my small video camera. Not for long. I was pounced on by the police and arrested on suspicion of being an organiser of the fracas. I spent the second half locked up, but when the match ended I was released and managed to link up with the ICF as they made their way out of the ground.

Given our modest numbers, it was important to stay close and not become isolated. Sure enough, as we crossed the bridge over the River Trent, I could see a large gathering of 150 Nottingham boys waiting. The sparse West Ham contingent was being escorted by eight stern mounted police, who seemed keen to get the Cockney bastards out of town.

With home advantage the Nottingham boys knew when and where to strike, and as the ICF filed past exchanging pleasantries the local crew suddenly surged across an area of derelict ground, grabbing up rocks and bricks and hurling them at us as they advanced. Our meagre group stayed tight but we were quickly backed up against two advertising hoardings that formed a shallow 'V' behind us. My camera stayed in its bag. We were set up like coconuts in a shy, and as the fusillade began the mounted police evaporated. Crouching in a kind of upright foetal position, I tried to make myself as small as possible. As I peered up from beneath my arms, I took a brick on the shoulder. This was going to end badly.

Then I saw Gardner. 'Stand, stand!' he roared. Flanked

by Swallow and Big Ted, he walked into the hail of bricks. They were all hit. Swallow sustained a head wound and Gardner a cut below the eye. This didn't stop them and they edged forward, snarling and sneering at the opposition, who began to back off. That defiant manoeuvre broke up the intensity of the attack and gave the rest of us the chance to slip away sideways.

But now the police were back, and although their presence kept the Nottingham posse at bay they harassed us all the way back to the train station. My impression was that they were very happy to see a bunch of Cockneys on the wrong end of a cascade of bricks.

Bill Gardner, over 20 years ago: loyal, bold and unflinching. I was grateful to him that day.

Acknowledgements

For all the people that stood with me and for the people that stood against me. With further thanks to all my family for standing by me all these years.

CHAPTER ONE

BOYHOOD TO TEENS

My name is Bill Gardner. In 1986 I was arrested for being 'The General' – the leader of the ICF, who were the hardest gang of football fans England has ever produced. This is my story. A story of friendship, pride, honour and trust – things that have disappeared from our society today.

I will tell you things that you may think are lies, but, believe me, they happened. At the end of reading my book, I will leave it up to you to decide if I was a hardened criminal or merely a man with a love of football and his chosen club.

I was born on 29 January 1954 to Bill and Charlotte Gardner in Hornchurch, Essex. My dad was a Ford car worker, my mum a shop assistant. Both were originally from the East End. My childhood was a very unhappy time. My parents never got on and were constantly fighting. Through the whole time I never once saw my father hit my mother; it was always the other way round. I remember times when I would cower under the settee if they were at it.

But I loved football and, even though I was not particularly good at it, I had trials at Fulham as a youngster. I first started going to football with my father at Tottenham. He was an avid Spurs supporter and I think he would have liked me to support his team too. Going to football was the thing to do back then, although speedway was also popular. These were the days when the insurance man knocked at the door, days when you had shilling, two bob meters for electricity, a rental TV, an HMV gramophone cabinet, big black telephones... and football, football, football.

I was fortunate that in those days, when Tottenham played away, West Ham would be at home. So my father would take me along to West Ham every other week. Tottenham had all the appeal with players like Danny Blanchflower, Dave Mackay, Bobby Smith and Cliff Jones, who cemented their place in football history by winning the league and FA Cup double in 1960/61. They were truly the glamorous side of the day, but I still looked forward to going West Ham. It had a great family atmosphere and I felt at home there. West Ham was like the family I'd never really had.

Unless you knew my background you would find this strange, but throughout the years I've always felt that way about it. Even when I've been at grounds in later life, when I've looked at the team's supporters it hasn't been as West Ham fans, or even as friends; I've always looked at them as my family and have taken it upon myself to look after them.

By the time I was 14 or 15 years old I was hardly ever in school. It wasn't because I wasn't clever – I used to get above-average marks in exams – but school was just something that I wasn't interested in. I used to drive a lorry with some gypsy mates. I was driving lorries at 14; I know I shouldn't have been, but I was, and that was the only way I could earn any money to feed myself. I spent nearly a year of my life on the road, homeless and sleeping in doorways, and it taught me to be a man. You learn to grow up quickly being homeless in London. It was one of those painful periods of my life that I try to block out, and I still don't like thinking about that time.

The problems at home didn't get any better, with everyone at each other's throats, and in the end my mum kicked me out. I suppose nowadays people would say that the beatings I took as a child were a sort of abuse. My mum used to beat me with a broom handle, which she broke over me several times. My dad sawed it off and put a grip on it so it was like a Japanese riot policeman's baton. We used to have the old butler sinks in them days, and they had a plastic bit over one end. It really hurt if you were hit with that. I don't believe I was a naughty child. I never got in trouble with the police. I had a few tear-ups at school but nothing too great. Like I said, my mum was the fiery one in our house, and perhaps our personalities never mixed.

As I got older, as much as I still loved her, I couldn't wait to get away from home. I got married when I was 17 partly to escape the life we had at home. But we were too young and we never got on that well. We split up after a couple of years, which meant walking away from my daughter Kelly when she was a baby. I took the decision then that it would be better if I didn't keep going round, as it would only upset her when I left. I thought it would be best if I just went away and kept away. It was a decision I took as a young man and one that I now regret. Kelly's now got a lovely little daughter called Macey and a really nice feller called Noel. I would have loved to make friends with her, but I think too much water has gone under the bridge now. We did try but it didn't work out for us. But the door's still open so you never know.

Christmas Day was never a celebration in our house. My childhood memories of Christmas are of my parents fighting and my mum giving my dad a good clump. My dad would never hit her back, but she would smack his face and throw his presents at him. She had a boyfriend for over 30 years, Edward, who we used to call Uncle Ted, and she used to go over to his house on Christmas Day and cook the dinner over there as it was only 100 yards away. Then she'd bring dinner home for my dad and me on a tray. This obviously used to upset my dad, but when he said something she'd attack him.

My mum was West Ham through and through. She was born in Chris Street, Poplar. She might have looked a bit frail but she would fight anybody. Even in her later years nobody would take the piss out of her. I inherited her aggression for sure. Once she walked out of hospital following a major operation after attacking the nurses. I love my mum to death and I stuck with her to the bitter end, but my memories of childhood are not what other people have.

I had a sister who died of leukaemia four years before I was born, and I don't think my mum and dad ever got over her death. I think when they had me they hoped I would be a cardboard cut-out of my sister, but when big, ugly me came out I wasn't quite what they wanted. I know my dad had a nervous breakdown when my sister died, and I think I never really got into the equation. My dad only ever saw me play football once when I was 26 years old. It was the last real game I ever played. I stopped playing through injury as I suffered five broken legs in my football career. But I did manage to score in that game and that pleased me.

So I guess you could say I was always a loner. That was why I was a bit peeved when I was arrested and they said I was a member of the ICF. Sure I went around with people that were part of the ICF, but I never regarded myself as being in the group. I've always been me. I don't need a gang, I don't need other people, I'm my own person, and that's all I ever was.

Other people, other fans, look at West Ham as the ICF, but I only see West Ham. I never saw the ICF. Leaving calling cards never really appealed to me; cutting people up never appealed to me. There were times when I had to use something in my hand to defend myself from people using weapons. Like when there was a shooting incident in Spain. At times I had to fight for my life and, if they had a weapon, I had to have a weapon. But if the man wanted to fight me with his hands, then I would do the same. These were wild times: football violence was kicking off everywhere. It was part of the going; it was a way of life. Most people from that generation, the 1970s and 1980s, don't call it football violence. It was a way of life. It was different back then.

Today football violence is played out by people who would be fighting in clubs or pubs if they weren't doing it at the football. But at the football they know that there are other people there like them. They want a tear-up and they know they'll get one at the football. But today's lot are not worth anything. I don't rate any of them. They're mugs. They don't love the team. West Ham United is my life. I wouldn't have fought anybody for any reason other than West Ham United.

People who know me know I'm not a violent person, but when somebody winds me up about West Ham I become a different type of animal. I've been told I've got a split personality, and perhaps this is what comes out of me when I'm at football. There's a kind side of me that loves pets and kids. People that have known me well have said that I'm two people: the person that a lot of people seem to like, and this person that erupts inside me – the person who I don't like.

When I was a child at primary school, I was always bullied. I was the little fat kid who used to get pushed off his chair and would have food thrown at him at dinnertime because he was a loner. I remember one particular person who went to my primary school used to bully me all the time. I remember I met him when I was 18 and said, 'Hello, mate, do you remember me?'

And he said, 'No, sorry, I don't.'

And I said, 'I used to sit next to you at school.'

And he said, 'Oh, yeah, I remember Billy Gardner.'

And before he could get another word out I'd flopped him and knocked him out. When he came to I said, 'Now you remember who I am, for all the bullying you done at me, that's what you get.' I never forget; I'm like an elephant. Somebody treads on me, I make sure I get them – it's as simple as that. Nobody will ever get away with it with me. To have me, you've got to kill me, because in the end I'll get people back who hurt me. They will pay the price.

I was very lacking in confidence as a kid, so much so that my GP recommended that I have hypnosis. I was one of only two people in England to have hypnosis from Dr Brown, who had a surgery in Hornchurch. In a very short time he gave me all the confidence I've ever needed. It's something I've never lacked from that moment on. I've got up and spoken in front of several hundred people at football functions. I've spoken on radio programmes. I find it very easy to talk now, and I've got loads of confidence. Dr Brown changed my life around from being the kid that was bullied to the kid that stuck up for himself. I hate bullies and I think that's what's driven me all these years. I can't stand big mouths talking about what they've done and what they're going to do. All the hard people I've ever met in my life have been quiet people – nice, kind people. But when you wind them up, that's when you stand out of the way, and that's what I think people know of me: that I'm a kind, caring person until you cross me, and then my split personality comes into it. It's something I've had under control now for many years, but it was a big problem when I was younger.

By now I'd discovered that I could hold my hands up, so I thought I'd try boxing. I trained for four years and won all of my six fights. But I couldn't get opponents because of my size and my age. At 16 I was offered the chance to become a sparring partner for a group of pro fighters. I was paid 20 quid a night, four nights a week. It was a great deal of money when my take-home pay for working in a factory was only seven pounds, eighteen shillings per week. I embarrassed well-known names of that era, but I don't want to say who in this book. Boxing taught me discipline and respect for other people, and that stands me in good stead even to this day.

They say I got my strength from another Bill in the

family: my Uncle Bill. He was the person that I took after most in my family. I was fiercely proud of Uncle Bill, who was the black sheep of our family but had a really colourful past. He was a stevedore on the docks and he told me stories from during the war when he had to go up to Newcastle and unload ships. The London dockers used to wear peaked caps with razor blades stitched into them as the Geordies were always having a go at them. But Uncle Bill never needed to do this because he was a circus strong man. His party pieces were lifting a grand piano above his head or lifting two 12-stone men sitting in chairs. He'd pick them up by the back leg of the chair and lift them above his head.

He also played football in the wartime league as a left-back. He was a ferocious competitor and a born winner. He died as he had lived, rushing with his Zimmer frame, trying to beat an old dame to the toilet in an old folks home. The two of them crashed and he came off his Zimmer frame and ended up dying. He'd had all of these big battles in his life and ended up getting done by a woman on a Zimmer frame! It never ceases to amaze me that even at his old age – I think he was about 90 when he died – he still wanted to beat somebody to the toilet. But he was a real character. Everyone hated him in my family, except me. I loved the old boy.

My Uncle Bill told me a story once from when he was at school and he was busting to go to the toilet. The teacher told him he couldn't go, so he just got up and pissed in all the ink-wells in the class. It always made me laugh as a kid when he told me that, because he just didn't give a damn. He used to tell me about how they used to unload bananas when they were working on the docks, and these spiders the size of your hand would crawl all over them. You don't hear many stories like that any more.

The name Bill Gardner means a lot of things to a lot of different people. A lot of people said to me that I was the top man at West Ham when I was 18, and I packed up when I wanted to pack up. Nobody retired me; it was as simple as that. I never felt I was a personality and I never wanted to be one. It's taken me years to do this book. I've never found it easy talking myself up. I never regarded myself as anything other than one of the lads. But in the last three or four years people have started coming up to talk to me and wanting me to sign autographs. I find it really strange because I'm just me. To my girlfriend Sarah I'm the same old Bill that she met all those years ago, and when my little boy James was born I decided that that was the end for me and I retired. I decided then that I would have no involvement in anything: no dodgy dealings and no violence whatsoever. I didn't want my son to grow up without a dad.

But before then there was the odd incident or two…

CHAPTER TWO

STAND, WEST HAM, STAND!

WEST HAM v CELTIC, 1967

One of my early memories is from when West Ham played a testimonial for Bobby Moore against Celtic. I think it ended 3–3. The ground was packed solid with fans. Over the years I've come to know quite a few Celtic fans and a couple of times they have come with us to away games. And they're all right, nice fellas. But that day, that testimonial game, was unbelievable. It was played like a European Cup match. It was a great atmosphere, but there were just so many of them. There were as many Celtic fans as there were of us, maybe more. They were everywhere. It was quite common for a Scottish club to be chosen as the opposition for testimonials, because in those days they always used to come to London in huge numbers. I remember going to see Queens Park Rangers play a Scottish side at Loftus Road and there were loads of fans there. They come and make a weekend of it.

A lot of the Celtic fans were loaded with whisky, and there were whisky bottles, half bottles and bottles of lager everywhere. It was unbelievable. But it went off quite a lot. I was in the North Bank that night. There were only a tiny amount of us in there and we were surrounded by Celtic fans. They had fantastic support that night, that's for sure. I think, if I had to say, that was probably the biggest and best mob that ever came here.

In those days you couldn't get out to go to the toilet and everyone used to have to do it where they were standing because there was no way you could move. It was unbelievable. Rivers of urine would surge down the terraces, and you had to make sure your pockets were sewn up or somebody would piss in one of them. It was terrible.

The other time I remember a huge mob of away supporters was when we played Man United in 1967 and they won the league. We were at home and they still beat us 6–1. They had a fantastic amount of support that night. They were all throwing bottles of light ale at the little bar in the North Bank. I just remember there was beer all over the place. That's the only time they ever brought a mob down to our place. They can say what they like but I've got no reason to lie. That was the only time that they seriously came down. To be fair, they were that good a side that a lot of West Ham supporters didn't come because they didn't want to see us get beaten, so there were more tickets available for United.

That was when you'd just show up and pay at the turnstiles. The queue would stretch for miles at any big game. The queue for a ticket in the Main Stand used to start forming at 8.45 in the morning. I used to queue up for every other home game, alternating with an old boy from Dagenham, and I'd save him a place. He was on his own and so was I. That way I was always first in the queue and I used to get Row A, Seat 1, which is the end seat in the West Side Upper, right in the corner by the North Bank, level with the corner flag. I used to have that seat at every home game for about two or three years.

PORTSMOUTH v WEST HAM, c 1970

I remember we played Pompey in a friendly at Fratton Park in the late-1960s or early-1970s. I remember going down there on the train. Portsmouth had a big reputation as a mob – it was a bit like West Ham – and they really did stick by each other. I heard lots of people say that they were a ferocious mob. There was a lot of apprehension on the train going down there. When we got to the railway station they were waiting outside. It was in the days of the skinheads, and there were people wearing Trilbies who were into Ska music and all that sort of thing. And it went right off. We were lucky to keep our heads above the ground that day. I remember we walked down a road that leads alongside the ground that we called Dog Shit Alley, because there was just so much of it down there. I think that's what everyone has called it for years. But we really had to have our wits about us that day. I've got a lot of time for Portsmouth. They're nice people. They've always stuck by each other and that's good enough for me.

We used to have a West Ham supporter called Pompey who came all the way up from there to support us. And a few Pompey would turn up when we played Southampton. They hate Southampton with a passion. I've never been enthused about Southampton, that's for sure. But, like I say, I've always had a lot of time for Portsmouth. Their fans always get behind their team. Whenever you watch it on the television now, even though they haven't been doing that well in the Premiership, you always hear them singing right to the end.

DERBY v WEST HAM, 1970/71

We had a fair little team in 1970. I liked the team and I liked the way we played football. We went up to Derby that year and won 4–2. I remember coming out the ground and walking back to the station from where the old Derby ground was. With the new ground you have to go all round the houses to get to it. But to get to the old Derby ground you just walked through an estate where the houses were all boarded up to stop anyone smashing the windows. It was an unbelievable sight. Every single house had boarded-up windows. They must have had some nightmares there, but it was never West Ham's way to smash things up.

This particular time, as was often the case, as I didn't know many people, I was on my own. I began walking towards the station and there were about 20 other West Ham fans, mostly a lot older than me, who I just toed along with. One of them was Old Fred. A lot of people remember Old Freddie. He used to stand at West Ham always wearing his old donkey jacket, so some people called him 'Donkey Jacket' Fred. Old Fred could hold his hands up, there's no doubt about that. And I remember as we turned the corner into Station Road there was a load of Derby supporters waiting for us at the bottom near the station. There must have been 200–300, and only about 20 of us. Here we go, I thought. I was not that old and I figured I should just keep my eyes on the others to see what they would do.

Fred barked out the orders and we listened. 'Right, stretch out across the road and keep walking,' he said. And we walked towards them. 'Don't run towards them,' he said, 'because we'll lose energy, and by the time we get there we'll be knackered. Just keep walking. Show no fear, and as we go towards them watch their faces.' We literally filled up the road one abreast and I was on the right side of the group. To be fair, I thought we were going to get mullered. They stood there and watched and I don't think they could believe it. Here was our little mob coming down the road, outnumbered by about 10 to one, and we just kept on coming. We got to within 60 yards of them and then Fred said, 'Right, let's start trotting.' We started jogging towards them and I've never seen such fucking fear and panic in a group as I saw in this mob. Most of them turned and shot away, but some of them stood. Obviously, if they'd all stood there, they'd have murdered us, but they didn't have the bollocks. We got into them and I remember I saw Fred take down at least two or three, and I thought, This is the firm to be with.

I remember going home that night thinking we had been very lucky but that I'd met some really unique people and I'd learned a lot of things. I learned that, if you can keep your cool and not panic and you can hold your own, you will do well. Otherwise you'll get slaughtered. Nowadays you go to football and there are people trying to bring the football hooliganism back into the game. It's like they're trying to invent the wheel – somebody's already done it before and it still turns the same way round. So nobody's going to imitate what we did. But you learn things as you go: you learn not to stand in the middle of the road, you learn to stand by a wall, you learn to be with people you can trust and rely on, you learn that you only get respect if you give respect, and that's something I've always done. You have to earn respect; it's not something that's just given. It's nobody's divine right. It's something you earn, and I believe that over the years I've earned it.

But that Derby game was unbelievable and it was one of the things that stuck in my mind for years. That was the first time I smelled the fear in people. I looked at them, and three-quarters of them turned and shot away. And the ones who were standing, you could see them looking and wondering if they should stay or go. We had them in two minds. We just kept going – we knew that there was no option for us; we had to keep going to get into the station, otherwise we couldn't get home. So we steamed right into them.

We got back from Derby on one of the football special trains they used to lay on for the fans. Derby was always an easy station to bunk out of, and I think I bunked it that day by getting under the chair or the table as we used to do. You would hide until you got there and then get out through where they used to deliver the newspapers and the post. I did it a lot in those days because I was only young. I used to hitchhike quite a lot too. None of us liked hitchhiking but it had to be done, as there wasn't the money about in those days. I used to leave on a Friday night and bunk the train to Mill Hill Broadway. Then I'd walk from Mill Hill Broadway to Scratchwood Services and hitch a lift from there.

This unique group of West Ham lads were, like I say, a lot older than me. I was only a kid of 16 years old. It wasn't a bad night because I also lost my cherry. I think a lot of people in that little group thought, Hold on a minute, this kid's all right. He's not shit himself, he's not been a back marker, he's not been the water boy. I've been trying to remember exactly who was there – there was Fred, some of the old Mile End boys, some old lads from West Ham. I think the ones that were there will recall it, but all that sticks in my mind is Fred. He was an awesome man, and I'm sad to say that he's passed away. I will miss him but will never forget him.

NOTTINGHAM FOREST v WEST HAM, 1971/72

We always used to lose 1–0 at Forest, always to a penalty, and it was always scored by the same bloke – Ian Storey-Moore. Forest was one of the toughest places to go at the time, because we were all skinheads in London while they were all greasers or rockers and they were always up for it. Our firm at the time was really young – we're talking 16- to 19-year-olds – and we were up against 25- to 30-year-olds. It was tough. When you went to Forest you knew you were in for a tough time. I always used to get the boys to walk in the middle of the road. If you were in the middle of the road, you knew you were 20–25 yards from the river, and that was good enough for me. I always had a lot of time for Forest – they would always fight fair and never came tooled up. They threw a few bricks and that, but I never saw knives or anything that shouldn't have been there. And when we used to give them a beating they'd always take it like a man. To be fair, they held their own on more than enough occasions.

That year I was with a lot of the younger Mile End lot and there were about eight of us hitching a lift. That particular night the Windsor chapter of the Hells Angels came into the Scratchwood Services. They used to come in there for a cup of coffee and a burger. For anyone who doesn't know, the Windsor chapter was one of the hardest Hells Angels groups in the country. A lot of them got shot in the New Forest in a gang war related to drugs. So there we were, this young group of skinheads, and their lot were all over 30. At first there was no problem, but then it just all went off. The broom cupboard was quite near, which came in handy, because all these brooms, mops and buckets came out. We fought for our lives against this lot. Someone must have phoned the police, as they arrived quite quickly. We hid in the grounds in the bushes and the Hells Angels all sodded off on their bikes.

We met them at a later date and they were all right with us. This time they were there first and we walked in. I thought, Oh blimey, we've done it again. But there weren't so many of them. And one of them, I'll always remember, was a muscular geezer wearing a short leather jacket, with loads of tattoos and a goatee beard. He looked like something out of ZZ Top. He acknowledged us and as we sat down he came over and said, 'You lot showed a lot of bollocks the other week and we give you respect where respect's due.' I was a bit sad to hear that a lot of them got shot in the New Forest because they showed honour and courage. And they're the two most important things as far as I'm concerned. If you haven't got those two you're not even worth being a man.

But the first time we met them after that little trouble we managed to get a lift in the back of a caravan that was being towed by a builder. He bought the caravan as a tea hut for his workmen and he had it on the back of a trailer. We asked him for a lift to Nottingham and he put two in the front of the cab and I think there were six or seven of us in the back and we covered ourselves up with newspapers.

It was pissing down with rain. A couple of hours later as day was breaking he stopped and said, 'Right, this is it, lads.' We walked across the road and there was a sign saying Nottingham was 10 miles. The road I'm talking about is across the Leicestershire and Nottinghamshire borders and there's one particular house there whose postcode is a mixture of the two – the house is literally on the border of Leicestershire and Nottinghamshire.

We went into a little village and asked them if they had a bus that could take us to Nottingham, but they told us there was only one and we'd missed it. So we walked to Nottingham along the River Trent and it took us three hours. We were knackered. We'd walked three hours, we'd been in the back of a trailer, we were wet, we were cold, we were hungry, we were skint and we were kids. So we sat on a wall at the end of the Trent Bridge, all feeling fucked.

And all of a sudden this big mob of Forest came across the Trent Bridge. And when I say a big mob, there must have been 300–400 of them, and we had no chance. It was either run or get mullered. And as much as they're lads, my lot were fucked and they didn't want to run. And I said, 'You fuck off and I'll try and hold them back. I'll try and draw their attention, because I can't run. I'm absolutely fucking bollocked. If I run, they'll catch me in two seconds, so what's the point? You fuck off and I'll see if I can hold them.' I believe some of the lads that were there were looking back and saw what I did.

There was no traffic on the road, so I got in the middle of

the road and walked towards them. I thought to myself I'm going to get slapped straight away here. But they parted. The Forest fans parted and let me walk right through the middle of them. Nothing was said. They just kept walking and I just kept walking. And I thought I'd got away with it. I got to within about four rows from the back of them and a couple of them steamed into me. I took a couple of whacks to the head, but I didn't go down, and a couple of other Forest lads stepped in saying, 'Stop it, stop it, he's got more bollocks than you'll ever have.' And they just fucked off and kept moving and left me alone. One of the lads that stopped it said to me, 'You are either the bravest person I've ever seen or the biggest fucking idiot. But whatever, you have got bollocks and we respect you for that. And because you showed us respect up here today against us, come in the Trent End with us.'

My eye was a bit swollen and I had a couple of cuts on the side of my face, but I walked with them. After you cross the Trent Bridge you turn left down to the ground, and back then their end was formidable. West Ham only ever went in there once and it was a hard one. As I got to the gates I told them I was going to go in with my mates and they understood that. I nipped round the other end and I found my mates were all right. So at the end of the day I only took a couple of blows, my mates didn't get done, and for me the day was a result. We still lost to a fucking penalty – Frank Lampard Senior gave it away as I remember. Ian Storey-Moore banged it in and we had our usual away defeat. And we bunked back on the train.

In those days we had nothing like the fancy clothes and the smooth look that came later. We went to football and watched West Ham United and, if it went off, we were there and that was it. Nobody innocent got hit. I can't think of a single occasion in all the time that I've been watching that innocent people got clumped. The only people who ever got hit were people who wanted to clump you. So if that's such a bad thing, then so be it. But if somebody wants to clump me or wants to clump my mates, I'll be only too happy to oblige.

The Forest Trent End was always a hard place. We got through the turnstiles one year, probably some time in the 1970s because I was wearing jeans, shirt and Dr Martens, and they were wearing wide-bottom trousers, silly jackets, tank tops, long hair, moustaches and were all scarved up. I remember when a mate of mine, a Tottenham fan, went up there and they had a big row outside. They took his sheepskin, his Dr Martens and his Ben Sherman off him, and he came home in borrowed clothing apart from his shorts, pants and socks. They threw all his clothes in the river! It could be a very grim place to be. But we always used to hold our own in the road with them. Everyone knew the score and we made sure we were never in that position. Sometimes these things can happen to you if you put yourself in that position, but, if you're a bit wise, you don't let that happen. But getting in that Trent End was a different kettle of fish.

That year when we tried it, we walked through the

turnstiles and they were waiting for us. I remember I got caught in between the turnstiles and we had to fight for our lives to get out of there. We came a cropper that day. And all respect to them. There were some really close shaves, and Derby and Forest were places that you never went and sniffed at them. It was not easy. Some 40 or 50 West Ham made the move to get in the Forest end. We took people there that didn't even want to go in with us. People stuck together because they were mates, even though a lot of the people that were with us couldn't hold their hands up for toffee apple. But what they had was big hearts, and I'd rather have a big-hearted lad with me than a flash harry. That meant a lot to me, and I know people like Stevie Vaughn would stay with me till I'm dead, and you can't praise somebody like that enough. And Ted would never leave you. He would never leave a man down. And when you've got people like that around you, even if you're confident, you take more confidence from it because you know they're going to be there and they know you're going to be there. It's like you feed off each other and you're one big family. These are my family.

MAN UNITED v WEST HAM, 1971/72

I was in the Stretford End on the day George Best scored a hat-trick and our own Best, Clyde Best, got one back for us. It ended 4–2 to Manchester United. I was with some of the lads from Mile End. We had the normal sort of conversation about whether we should go in there and have a pop at them. I don't remember suggesting it, but somebody must have done. They said, 'Right, we're going in the Stretford End,' so in we went. It was all the usual mob that used to have a go: Joey Williams, Greeney, I think Billy Gall was with us, Kaydee, Sinclair, Alex and Jamie Anderson. And some people might remember Jeffrey who used to sell programmes at West Ham wearing a leather coat. Why in the hell he ended up with us, I'll never know. The poor sod got carried out on a stretcher.

I remember that day well. We went in through the turnstiles in ones and twos and made our way to the middle. They didn't suss us for a little while. They wouldn't know, would they, as they're all just odd-jobs up there. You could come from anywhere and be a United supporter. So we walked into the middle and just stood there. West Ham came out for a warm-up and we cheered them as they came up the tunnel. And that's when it went mental. They were all over us like a rash. It was a complete nightmare, I'll admit, but I wasn't going to stand there and be fucking quiet when the team came out. Nobody else had ever done it before, so we used to set records in those days. The team never used to, but we did. That Stretford End, they couldn't believe it, they were totally shocked. There were fucking hundreds of the bastards everywhere. We did all right. I think Jeffrey was the only one who got hurt. We stuck tight. We made sure that we all had our backs to each other. Anyone went down, we picked them up. It was a good little team we had there.

Because the lads were all straight, there were no

weapons used. They were all old school. Old school don't use a weapon – you don't need to walk around with a knife like some of them do now. There was no need for that. If you were good with your hands, you had a row. If you weren't, you didn't have a row. And we respected the people that didn't have a row in our group as much as the ones that did. Because the ones that couldn't have a row still had big hearts.

We were always looking down, so we must have been quite high. And they were all round us. I couldn't believe how many there were. We were whacking them, but they just kept coming, and coming and coming. And I think, because there were so many of them, half the time they hit each other rather than hit you. But all you have to really do is face the one who's immediately in front of you. And once he's out of the action, then you face the next one that's immediately in front of you. You must never take your concentration off the one who's immediately in front of you. If you look to the sides, that's when you get a slap. The one in front of you is the one you take out first. Once he's gone you take out the next one in the middle, providing you haven't let them close round you. Always keep to the middle. And, if you go through the middle, they always separate, and that's what they used to do in those days.

I think the Old Bill never expected anyone to do what we did, so they weren't prepared for it. There were a few there, but they were all at the front on the pitch. There weren't many police in with the supporters in those days because they were all Man United fans. There was no reason to. But, like I say, we had a right tear-up in there that day. The few police who were around were really quick. They got in there and they took us up into the corner of the Stretford End where they kept us and surrounded us. Loads of United were there ready to have a pop. They didn't stop trying to get at us, but I never got any of the 'Gardner, you're this and that,' because they didn't know me in those days. I was just a West Ham supporter. So it was 'Cockney cunt' and 'West Ham wanker' and all the usual shit you got.

We were surprised they didn't take us all out and around the pitch. If I had been the Divisional Police Commander there, I would definitely have said, 'Take the boys out.' I was quite hoping we would be, but we weren't. We stayed there in the wings and I remember that they kept us there till the end of the game and that was it. They gave us an escort out up to the little station. Nothing happened there. None of them came into us. Nobody made any move to us on the way back to the station at all.

I remember when we got on the train there was no room to sit down so we were sitting in what used to be the postman's cage. And there was the usual load of Man United supporters from London on the train. Today you'd get a fair amount of families going up for the game, but in those days the ones that used to go were there for a tear-up. And I remember that one of this little gang got real gobby and one of our lads called Greenie had a straightener with him in the cage and give him a right mullering. But, when it was all over, that was it. Nobody was cut or stamped on. In those days, you beat the man and that was the end of it.

WEST HAM v STOKE, LEAGUE CUP, 1972

Stoke was always a hard one, a bit like Forest were at that time. You always went up there and had a row. They were always game and still are from what I can make of it from people who still go now. We've had some battles with Stoke because we played them about a thousand times in the League Cup. I remember a lad got hit with a cricket bat in the toilets in the first leg of the semi in 1972 when we lost 2–1. And I remember that night on the way back to the station they came up behind us and there were loads of them. A few of us picked up lumps of wood and it went right off. We did all right. When they attacked us in the street I whacked one of them with one of those knob-shaped handles you get on trains and then I did a hasty retreat down the road while they were helping him up with his nose all over his fucking face. That was grim. But they'd already put one lad in hospital with a cricket bat. How you can take a cricket bat into a football match is beyond me, but they did. A big fight erupted because in those days you all shared the same toilet.

As I've said, I've got a lot of time for Stoke because they always put up a show and 99 per cent of the time they fought fair, but this particular time they had weapons. We had some right battles with them throughout the years and I remember one particular game in the 1983/84 season when we lost 3–1. Either we missed the train or the van broke down, but I remember we ponced a lift with a newspaper van. In those days they used to print the papers in London and take them up north in vans. The van was on its way back and we said to this bloke, 'Look, there's 11 of us, can you take us back to London if we pay you?' And he said, 'Yeah, all right.' So we give him £3 each to take us back to London, which was still fair going in those days. He opened the back of his van and it was just steel walls and floor with lumps of string on the side that had been used to hold the papers together. We ended up tying each other to the walls so we could go to sleep without falling over because it was so slippery. It was the only thing we could do, but if somebody had opened the back of the van it would have looked like a scene from *Dr Who*. The bloke dropped us off at Edgware on the underground that morning. It was another night when we stuck together – literally.

My other memory of our encounters with Stoke was again in the League Cup when we played them at Old Trafford. It was a horrible night. We had tickets but the police wouldn't let us in the end where we were supposed to be, so we had to jump over the turnstiles at the side of the ground. If you imagine Old Trafford as it is now, we were standing to the left as you come out of the tunnel. It took four games to decide the outcome as it went to the second replay. I remember that a lot of West Ham fans didn't get there at all because the trains were disrupted. And I remember Bobby Moore went in goal and saved a penalty but they scored with the follow-up. That was Stoke's year, and they deserved to win that night and in the final against Chelsea. Stoke had great players back then. George Eastham was one of the best players I've ever seen.

After the game we came out and banged into them on the concourse where the Old Trafford shop is. All hell broke loose and a policeman grabbed on to me and went to put me in the van. But he couldn't open the door because there was so much going on, so he let go of me and said, 'Fuck off, I've got something else to do here.'

But it went off that night, big time. There were a lot of angry West Ham fans and I think even Stoke would say that. At the end of the game, Stoke sang 'You'll Never Walk Alone' and put their scarves above their heads like Liverpool used to in the Kop. It was the finest time I've ever seen it done and I've watched Liverpool do it lots of times at Anfield, but that night when Soke was in the Stretford End, that one they did was unbelievable.

COVENTRY v WEST HAM, 1972/73

We lost 3–2 at Coventry in the 1972/73 season and I remember the walk back to the station after the game. At Coventry to get from the station to the ground you go through an area called Highfields, which I guess is where the ground Highfield Road gets its name. This particular night there were seven of us walking back to the station. Two of the lads had actually moved up to Coventry from East Ham, and I got talking to one of them whose name was Lennie. He said he'd walk us back to the station. I was with Bob Brown from Dagenham, John Heritage from Barking, Mad Frankie from Leytonstone and a couple of others who I've not seen in a long time but I'd like to meet up with again.

As we walked back up the road this Lennie said to me, 'There's a mob of them following us up the road behind us.' I think there were about 15 or 20 of them following us. We kept walking but they were gaining on us, so we figured we'd have to make a stand or otherwise they'd be all around us. We went underneath a flyover that had a pub next to it and an alleyway down the side. By this time it must have been 9.40 at night and it was pitch dark. We let them catch us up by this pub and we stood there and we had it off. Lennie had thrown a brick at one of these Coventry fellas that caught him in the chest, and it was bad. I think the lad was on the verge of losing his life. And I remember this Lennie shit himself because he didn't want to be up on a manslaughter or murder charge. I think it appeared in his local paper that this kid was nearly killed, but he managed to survive. I never had any contact with him after that, but that was another night when we had to fight for our lives.

It was a common occurrence in those days. You had the choice: you ran or you stood. And, if you ran, most times you would have got done anyway. And anyone who knows my physique – I've never been a Linford Christie – can tell you it was a case of standing your ground for me. You learn the hard way. You had to learn to look after yourself in those days. It was not a case of turn the other cheek, walk away and hope it's not going to happen to you, because it would happen to you. In our group lots of innocent people got clumped. They were just out to watch the football. So you had to stick up for yourself and you had to stick up for the ones that couldn't because otherwise people would take the piss out of you. If you stuck together and had a go, you got respect, and that's how we did it. Sometimes it was hard, and sometimes it was easy.

That time at Coventry was hard, and I thought at one point it was going to come all on top as they outnumbered us two to one. There was no doubt they were game for it, because they wouldn't have kept on creeping up on us like they did. They must have trotted so they could get behind us. And I remember thinking we were about 400–500 yards from the station and that we weren't going to get there before they caught us up. And I thought, once we got nearer the station, there would be more of them waiting for us there so we might as well deal with this lot first and then face whatever's up the station. Like I say, we really had to fight for our lives, and they steamed in right outside the pub. Because it was a small area, they couldn't get sufficient numbers around us, so they could only come at us from one way. That's why we decided to do it there because a few of us could hold the alleyway against a lot bigger force. If we'd stayed in the road I think we'd have been done, but in this little area they literally had to climb over their mates to get into us. So, once we could do the ones at the front, that would bring the numbers down quite a bit and a couple of them didn't turn out to be as brave as they thought they were when they were coming up the road.

We used to go in their end at Coventry and it would always go off. One year it went right off down by the Highfields shopping centre, and I remember we had to go through a flower shop and out the back door because we were outnumbered by a gruesome amount. I jumped into the flower shop and the woman said, 'Can I help you?'

And I said, 'Yeah, you can, where's the back door?'

She said, 'It's back there.'

And about 30 of us traipsed through her flower shop and out the back door! Avis nicked a bunch of roses, but that was him all over. He took them home to his mum. But that was quite funny. The woman asked, 'Can I help you?'

I said, 'Yeah, you already have. Where's the back door?' And that was quality. She was a nice lady. Obviously, she was a bunch of flowers light, but that was the way it was.

MAN CITY v WEST HAM, 1972/73

Donald Francis noted in the book *Guv'nors*: 'The only firm that did it at Maine Road in the early days was West Ham.' Also, Tony O'Neill told in his book, *Red Army General*, of a handy firm of West Ham taking it to City in the Kippax.

Both these accounts, which are from different games between 1972 and 1974, stand up, though the Red Army General may be mistaken when he mentions an axe, and I can put this down to his age at the time.

Going to either of the two Manchester clubs as a West Ham supporter was at its worst in the early 1970s. Out of the two, it's City we rated more than United. I can't give you dates, but between 1971 and 1975 it was always a grim day out at Maine Road.

I remember one time two or three coaches left from Upton Park. Ours was a Lacey's coach and was the only one going on to Blackpool. I don't know who arranged it but the plan was to spend the night in Blackpool and see the lights. Plenty of lights that day, that's for sure. The spirit on the coach on the way was good even though West Ham never won many games away from home in those days. Away from home we'd have our regular three wins, five draws and the rest were all defeats. You know in yourself supporting West Ham that you don't go there for the glory, because there isn't any. Not for watching the team anyway.

We got up there with only enough time to get in the ground. I'm not one who likes to have a good drink before a game anyway. In those days they put us in the corner next to the Kippax where City's main supporters went. So when you came out you sort of mingled together and the coach park was right outside their end too. So it was always a lively place to go and, if you had your coach or your car parked anywhere away from the ground, you had to walk through all these little narrow streets and alleyways to get there. They would always be waiting for you. So the move is to be sensible, look after each other and stay close. You know the score. Never get caught out in the open. Stay by a wall so if it goes off you're only facing your enemy from one or two sides instead of three or four.

I was on my own when I came out. I don't know why, but I was left behind by the others. And all the little roads and the alleyways around that ground were a nightmare. I remember another year up there they captured us in the roads and people were running and screaming. We had some children with us and we had to get in people's back gardens. It was a nightmare. Obviously when you go away from home you're outnumbered heavily. Most times you're outnumbered at least 10 or 20 to one, and in those days we didn't take the numbers that people take away now. Now clubs take thousands away from home, but in those days sometimes you had 20 or 50, especially if it was a night game all the way up north.

Anyway, when I got back I saw a big fight had started in the car park near the coach. Two West Ham supporters were being attacked by about six Man City supporters. I went into the City supporters and managed to do three of them, while the other three ran. But in the process I broke my hand hitting one of them. That night we went to Blackpool for the night. And on the Sunday morning I was left in Oldchurch Hospital in Romford having my hand done. The two West Ham supporters I helped ran away and got on the coach. Nobody else on the coach got off to help me. My then wife-to-be, Leslie, was on board. She wanted to get off and help me. There were several other West Ham on there who said they tried to get off but they couldn't. But I was one of the last ones back on the coach and I saw this incident happen. To be fair, I would have gone to anyone's aid, no matter if they were a West Ham supporter or not. If people are being bullied like that, I'll help them.

A couple of years previous to that I'd gone up there and there were several of us in the Kippax. We had them all round us and, as it always happened in those days, a roar went up, a big circle appeared and we were stuck in the middle. I was with Mad Frankie, who was a good mate of mine at the time. There were about seven of us in our group, including Stevie Morgan's sister, and I think she was pregnant at the time. But she was a good one to have with you; she could row as well as any man. I've never discriminated between women and men. If they are brave enough to stand and have a row, they get my full respect. And it was as simple as that. She certainly got that because I thought she was quality.

The City lot were coming at us from all angles. A couple of us got kicked in the back. We turned round, had a pop and we stood. They started to say silly things and all the usual stuff you used to get up there. Anyone in those days knew as soon as they said to you, 'Have you got the time?' you didn't say anything. If you were going to clump them, you clumped them. Because once you told them the time and they knew where you came from, they were going to clump you. So I used to get in first – end of story. We were severely outnumbered just before the kick-off, and they had come into us a couple of times and we held our own.

And then they came in again about 25 minutes into the game. I saw the threat coming up towards us. I wanted to get down the front so that I could face them one way. I could see them coming from behind me, but they got into us and we had no chance. There were just too many of them. And if the Old Bill hadn't come in, I think then we'd have got a right hiding.

I remember the Old Bill had a word with me. They came round and got hold of me and said, 'We've been told you've got an iron bar in your newspaper.'

And I said, 'It's got some lead writing on it, but it's no iron bar,' and I just opened it up and showed them it was a newspaper.

The Man City supporters got a bit braver when they saw that. Everyone knows the newspaper trick. If ever you're on your own and you're a bit worried about what's going on, roll a newspaper up nice and tight and, if somebody comes at you, you have got something to hit them with. That newspaper rolled up is a beefy thing to hit someone on the head with. I rolled mine up very tight and I made them think that I had something in the paper, but I didn't. But they didn't want to take a chance.

Eventually we were causing so much trouble that the Old Bill slung us out. The police came in, pulled us on to the pitch and threw us off the Kippax. As they took us round the pitch all you could hear was 'We hate the Cockneys, we hate the Cockneys'. All the Kippax were pointing fingers at us and all that – the normal rigmarole they used to give you. They slung us out into the street and we decided we had to get back to Manchester Station. Our train wasn't until five-thirty and it was only about three-thirty at the time. We didn't think any City had come out after us, but when we walked up the road we noticed a few following us. We had a couple of little skirmishes with them. You know, you walk a little bit, you look in the shop windows as you walk past to make sure you're all right and everyone's with you. I've always walked at the back – it must be because I'm a slow walker – and I could see a few coming down the road behind us. Not too many of them, not too many dramas, but there were maybe about 11 or 12. The others had gone in the opposite direction because they had hired a private coach, leaving the seven of us to make the station.

But we were OK. They didn't have a pop until there were about 15 or 16 of them and they outnumbered us two to one. When they had their first pop, we beat them back. They hung back for a little while, and then they had another little go at us on the way to the station. But none of us got whacked or hurt. We got back in the station at something like 4.40, and I remember we were in the waiting area where the phone boxes are and a mob of them came in to have a go. There were a couple of our firm who were on the phone and they ripped them out and used the receivers to whack them with. Now there was a large amount of them in the station, I can assure you. It was like fucking Rorke's Drift; they never stopped coming. They were all over us and we were exhausted because we were fighting for our lives. And again, if it hadn't been for the police coming, I think it would have been the end of our lives. There were just too many of them.

The Old Bill put us on the train and we were all absolutely knackered. Stevie Morgan's sister was absolutely whacked. I haven't seen her for years, but I wish her well and I hope she knows I hold her in high regard. Same with Frankie from Leytonstone – I haven't seen him for years, but he was a real character with no fear.

These sorts of situations happened often, and anyone who went to football in those days knew the score. If you went, no matter what team you supported, you were going to get involved in trouble. If you came from London and you were going to the Midlands or the North, they singled you out. They wanted to fight you because they outnumbered you and I defy anyone who doesn't believe me, even the do-gooders who might say, 'Oh, yeah, the bloke's a fucking hooligan.' No, I'm no hooligan. I went there and I stuck up for myself. I always did and always will.

Looking back, Man City should be on our list of teams to hate, it was always a bad place to go, but truth be told I love Man City. Supporting Man City is like supporting West Ham – you're loyal, you get shit on year after year, but you always stick with the team. True Manchester people support Man City for me. Every Man City fan I've met has always been a genuine character. I think there's a lot of affinity between us and them. They were always pretty fair and I've got time for them. Not like the other mob. I can't bear the other mob. I've got a lot of mates who'll read this book who are Man United supporters and they'll think I'm slagging them off, but the ones I know aren't the ones that I deal with. As I've said, I only ever clumped people that wanted to clump me. I've never clumped an innocent person, or somebody with his kids or missus.

But I didn't have a lot of time for Man United because there were so many and they used to think they were the bee's knees. And to be fair, I never rated them. Never have, never will. Just because you outnumber people 30 or 40 to one, that doesn't make you a hard man. You could smell the fear in them when you faced them. That's one of the things I'll always remember. It's like a lion when he faces the wildebeest on the Serengeti plains. I could see the fear in their eyes and I knew we would be the winners. That isn't being flash; that's being truthful. The fear used to spread like wildfire, and I and all the other people with me used to feed on it.

WEST HAM v MILLWALL, 1970s

The best row I was involved with against Millwall was Harry Cripps's testimonial in 1972. Millwall had a lot of older guys and some of them still go now. You always knew you were in for a hard time over there. There were no easy rides. But that night we had the upper hand. Eleven times we steamed back into the ground and ran them. It was the worst trouble I'd ever seen at a football match and I've never seen it worse since. It was terrible. The atmosphere was hatred, real hatred. It was all about proving who was worst – them or us. They had a big mob with a big reputation. The build-up had been going on for weeks and everyone was up for it. Everybody who was anyone was there.

What people might not understand is that, apart from the tough mates you had around you, you also had a lot of people that weren't so tough. You had people that had other qualities. You had your planners, your organisers, your people that you couldn't rely on for rowing, but you knew that they'd be with you. There were people there that couldn't fight their way out of a paper bag, but you knew if you looked round and you were in the shit that they would still be there with you and they would take hidings for you. And in life that doesn't happen that often. Especially nowadays. That sort of thing's all gone. But that was a really big thing. We had a good firm out that day, that's for sure.

The Mile End boys were our top firm, but because I didn't come from there I didn't see them until the day. We met on the night and we knew it was going to be tough. There were never any thoughts of losing; it was just thoughts of who would get hurt out of our firm, and you had that in your stomach when you went over there. It was always a daunting place to go, and still is. They are the only mob that are like us. They stick by their mates and they turn out for the big games. They've got a lot of hangers-on now – the youngsters that are over there now are trying to make a name for themselves, but I'm afraid they're 20 years too late. It's all right inventing a new burger, but Wimpy and McDonalds did it years ago. It's as simple as that.

We got on the train at Mile End and went on the Underground through Whitechapel and came out at New Cross Gate Station. A full train load came out and some of theirs were waiting outside and got slapped. We walked down the road to the pub on the corner. It went off outside the pub and the atmosphere was pure hatred. There was no feeling like going down to the old Den ground of Millwall back then. It was a unique atmosphere, like a cold feeling in your bones. It was a survival instinct, like you'd get if you were left in the Sahara Desert with nothing to eat and no clothes on. I used to feel it every time we played: we must survive. It was grim.

They were just inside the pub and when they came out it all went off. You could hear the sound of beer mugs being broken in the pub as we charged. But there was just one charge before the police broke it up. We went into the game and you could tell by the atmosphere it was going to go off. Mile End stick together. Mile End didn't want anyone else with them. They didn't need anyone else with them. I give Millwall their due – they came for it, without a doubt. All of London was with them, and there was us, just on our own. To be fair, I knew that there were people in our mob that day that were worried.

First of all they were throwing abuse over to us, and you got the silly ones wearing surgical masks and all that. I don't know what that's supposed to do. That was the first time I'd seen people wearing surgical masks and I thought it was so funny because none of them could spell surgeon let alone be one. I just thought it was the funniest thing in the world to see these blokes walking around with surgical masks on. Was that supposed to frighten you? It didn't work with me. You either put up or you shut up. That particular day we were behind the goal and they were on the side. You could get all the way round in those days, but their mob stayed just a little bit off the halfway line throwing abuse at us.

The rivalry was nothing new – it goes back nearly 100 years. People from that part of London don't like people from our part of London. I hear stories of derbies, like Liverpool and Everton, where they are all mates and can go for a drink together after the game. That will never happen with West Ham and Millwall. Never.

All through the game they were throwing things – pennies, little bolts, ball bearings – all these little things that were heavy and would hurt if you got caught by one. Towards the end of the game we managed to slip out and get round and wait for them to come out. Everyone was there and prepared for it. There was nobody there just to shout and bawl; everyone was there and wanted it and it was a hell of a firm.

At the end they were all stood on the top of the stairs and charged down at us. We charged them back in 11 times as they tried to get down the stairs. After the game there was only one winner, and that was us. It was like if you hit form playing darts and you're whacking them in the treble 20 all the time and know you're never gonna miss. That's how we felt. We knew that we couldn't be beaten. We were top of our form and we knew we had them on the rocks. You could tell by the look in their eyes. You could see the fear and you could see that they didn't want to know that day.

There were more little isolated incidents. I saw a policeman taken off his horse. Somebody jumped up and hit him with a spanner. It was a great big thing used to bolt railway lines with. God knows how he lifted it, whoever it was. I saw that, and it was pretty grim. There were police horses charging down the road, treading on you wherever they could. But that day was all about us taking it to Millwall and it was the best victory we'd ever had over them, and I don't think we've ever had another one like that since.

In later years when we played them it was never quite the same. There was one other game, and why the clubs ever agreed to another testimonial was beyond me. I guess it was the money, as money talks in football. There's no consideration for people's safety. I think this other

43

testimonial was for a lad called Bobby Neil. We weren't many-handed and we'd gone in the Cold Blow Lane. Bunter was there, Ted was there, Tiny was there and I can't remember who else. Tiny was giving it loads of mouth like he's always done with me, and it all came on top. We were outnumbered by 30 or 40 to one at least, and at half-time we thought we'd better get out of there because it was getting on top. There was plenty of flex but no action.

The Old Bill got round us and at half-time we made our way down the stairs. As we were making our way down another load of them from the halfway line were coming up the stairs. I saw somebody had a meat hook under his coat, and I thought this was it. They looked at us, and we looked at them, but they didn't realise that we were West Ham. We got outside the ground and luckily enough nobody came out after us and we made our way back to the station. But that was as grim as it could get over there.

CARLISLE v WEST HAM, 1974/75

Carlisle was a bleak place. You saw the fans coming to the game by walking over the fields. We'd won 1–0 and wanted to get something to eat and drink before we got on the train. I was with my mate Ray, known as Curly, and another lad called Owen. Owen's dad at that time was the Mayor of East Ham and we've been mates for many, many years. Ted was with us too.

We went in the supermarket and as soon as we started getting our bit of grub together a load of Carlisle supporters came through the door. They'd watched us come into the supermarket and they'd followed us in. I don't know how many of them there were but there were only four or five of us. So it was action stations again. There was a broom cupboard that came in handy and I think I was pushing Ted around in a trolley while he wielded a broom handle. Two of our lot were throwing milk bottles from the back of the shop to the front, trying to get the Carlisle out. All I remember is slipping and sliding on a load of milk on the floor and trying to whack them with a broom handle. It was like something out of a Charlie Chaplin film. Every time you tried to move you were falling over because of the milk and we were giggling because it was so funny to be stuck inside using a trolley like a chariot with a broom handle. But I remember we chased them out of the shop, got our grub and went home. That was unbelievable.

You won't play at Carlisle today, as they are a non-league club. But, if you ever went there as a football fan, you would certainly remember the place and the sight of sheep everywhere. You were walking past the sheep on the hills to get to the ground. The train used to come in like you were in the Rocky Mountains in America. If you drove quickly from London and you only stopped once, it would take you five hours to get to Carlisle, and that's if you had a clear road. But in those days we went by football special and you could be leaving at eight in the morning and you'd get there at one in the afternoon. I swear they had square wheels some of those trains. And they certainly didn't have heating on them. Anyone who sat on them will remember that. The windows used to steam up in the winter and there was no food.

The policemen weren't too bad in those days – not like this current mob that couldn't catch a cold. They were half-decent blokes then that had respect, and we gave them respect back. Now it's not there; it's like the horse has bolted. Some of them I've met have been fair. Binsy, the West Ham spotter, he's all right. He's always been fair to me and the lads. We've always respected him and we get it back. I've never given him no grief, and he's never given me none. He knows that I'm retired now.

That said, I do still get problems with away Bill. I get the odd look and the odd comment. I ain't done nothing since 1984/85 and yet they still look out for me. I remember going to Southampton about five years ago. I walked down the road and a Southampton copper said, 'Hello, Bill,' just to let me know he knew who I was. And I thought, Do you want my fucking autograph or what? That's the way they are.

It was the same at Cardiff last season. I've got a bad leg and I couldn't walk the distance from Cardiff Station to the ground. I was at the back of the escort and got the usual push in the back to keep me moving. And I said to the copper, 'Look, I can't do it walking like this.'

And he said, 'Right, we'll give you a lift,' and they pulled up a van and put me in it.

It was quite an interesting journey back to Cardiff

Station. I could hear on the police radio all that was going on. The police surrounded all the West Ham supporters in what they call a 'bubble'. And they had snatch squads running in front of the bubble, going into the side roads and trying to clear the Cardiff fans.

I got talking to the policeman and he asked me if I had been going a long while, and I said, 'Yeah.' Then he asked me if I knew a few names, including my own. I said, 'Yeah, I know him well. It's me.' And I think I made his day.

He said, 'They won't believe me back at the station when I tell them I had Bill Gardner in the van with me.' And I signed a bit of paper for him with my autograph. He was a nice lad.

I've got nothing against the police – they do their job and I do mine. I've only got something against the lying bastards who tried to frame us up. They know who they are. They all thought they were something else but they didn't have a brain between the lot of them. And they paid the price with their jobs and the money that we got weighed out for compensation. If you're going to fix somebody up, try to do it properly. My family suffered, like everyone else's because of that. It's wrong to try to bang somebody up when they haven't done anything. If they're doing it, fair enough, but I hadn't been doing it then for a few years.

And what was I supposed to be doing? Not robbing banks, not knocking old women on the head, not mugging people. What I did was go to football, watch the team I love, West Ham, and, if somebody wanted to fight, I'd have a fight with them. It's as simple as that. I don't believe anything I did was wrong. I don't believe that the values that we showed during the time were wrong. I don't believe that showing courage and honour and sticking by your mates and being loyal is a bad thing. I just don't believe that. I think they're values that are totally missing in our society now. Nobody's loyal to their mates any more, nobody stays in their job; they all run away. Nobody shows any courage or chivalry, or has any honour any more. But we had it. It's a sore point with me and I could argue about it all night long.

WEST HAM v MAN UNITED, 1975

I think everyone had a coat or jacket they got fond of when going to football. My favourite was an old black coat. It was an old ambulance jacket and that coat alone could tell some stories. We were playing Man United at home in 1975 and we got to the ground really early. I think it was about nine in the morning. There had been a lot of chat from their lot about coming down and taking liberties, but that's not how it happened. They never showed or if they did it must have been very late. That was the usual thing when people came to West Ham. They'd come out of the station at 2.50, make as much noise as they could and get a police escort down to the ground. The police back-up got them through the many West Ham supporters waiting in the streets. So this was the Red Army that said they were going to come early. They would be down Friday night in those days. They used to go to London but they never used to go anywhere near us.

West Ham supporters have always gone early to places. You'll always see West Ham fans walking round at 12.30 or 1.00 at any ground you go to in the country, even now. Now that there's practically no trouble at football matches you'll see West Ham fans outnumbering the home fans early in the afternoon. But in those days any visiting fans went in the South Bank and some in the West Side. I was in the West Side when a fight started and there was one policeman standing near me. He was only a young lad and he was shitting himself. I had my black jacket on which made me look like I was one of them and I said to him, 'You all right, mate?'

He went, 'No, I'm petrified.'

And I said, 'It's all right, we're together, there's two of us. I'm plain clothes.'

And he said, 'All right.'

And I was talking to him all the time while it was going off. He was clumping West Ham supporters trying to keep them apart, and I was clumping the other lot.

I think somebody must have used the binoculars and thought, Hold on a minute, who's this one alongside our officer? Immediately a load of police came in, pinned me up against the wall and said, 'What are you doing?'

And the policeman said, 'No, he was helping me.'

And they let me go, which was handy. It's quite funny really, because when you get to talk to some of them they're only young lads who are doing their job, and he's a lad that got caught on his own. I don't think there's enough money in the world to make me do that job.

Another time I was with my second missus Janice and we were in the Sheffield United end at the back and they all got around us. I had a West Ham scarf on underneath my jacket. They came up at us, but what was in our favour was we were above them and we were facing down. I remember this big, stocky Sheffield bloke with a flat cap coming forward, and he was giving it large. He came forward and I hit him with the best punch I've ever caught anyone with in my lifetime. And he went down like a sack of spuds. He was out of the script. Two of them fell over him because he was on the floor. We just fought for our lives and everyone got split up. I went to the tea stall with Janice, and one Sheffield United supporter was talking to me quite a lot. You've got to bear in mind I'd just had a right tear-up and I was pretty knackered. And we were surrounded by them. This guy said, 'Give me your scarf.'

And I said, 'No, I'm not giving you me scarf. You want the scarf, you come and get it.'

And they tried, but luckily enough I got hold of the tea urn before they did and one of them got it on his head with no sugar.

Then the police came and took me down to the charging room, which used to be to the left side of the home end out in the car park, and this policeman said, 'Right, you stand in the queue.'

I had my black jacket on and I started thinking. So I took the West Ham scarf off before I went in, and I gave it about three minutes and just leaned forward and went, 'Righto, sarge, I'm going back on duty now, all right?'

And he went, 'Yeah, OK, mate,' and I just walked out and nobody came after me.

It was like chaos in that charging room. There was one sergeant sitting at the table and another officer sitting to his immediate right. But there were so many people in the queue they couldn't see what was going on at the back. And I was right at the back of that queue. I think when he saw the jacket, which even had the stripes on it, he automatically thought I was a policeman. So I just had the front to turn round.

Another time West Ham were playing Birmingham and the train lines went up the creek. We couldn't get further than Tring. So we thought we'd go to the Luton–Arsenal game instead. Some of the lads went in the away end and the word came around that West Ham fans were trapped in there. I went up to the police officer in charge who had, I think, two pips on his shoulder. I don't know what rank that is, but he must have been quite a high-ranking officer and was in charge of everything that was going on at Luton. I had a trilby on and this coat. I said to him, 'I'm up from London on surveillance and I'll go in there and get them out, because one of the lot I've been watching is in that mob in there.'

And he said, 'OK, what do you want?'

I said, 'I want four officers and a sergeant.' And he gave me them.

I went in the away end and all the boys were looking round laughing because I'm coming in with all these bobbies behind me and I'm telling them what to do. I managed to get the police around our lot, because they were outnumbered severely and they would have got a right pasting, and the police took them out. When we got outside they just dispersed, and as I walked away the policeman shouted out, 'Who are you with?' And I just turned round and tapped my finger to my nose as if to say, 'Ssh, you'll give me away.'

I think if you've got the front to do it, you can get away with anything. You have to believe what you're doing. If you believe in what you're doing, you can swing it. I didn't really want to go to Luton, I wanted to go home, but everyone went. The whole train load. So they got coaches and took us from Tring to Luton – what a crazy idea to ask West Ham fans where they want to go. Of course everyone thought, Arsenal's at Luton, so let's go there. That'd be a tear-up. They even hired coaches to take us. Three or four coaches pulled up within 20 minutes. From Tring in Hertfordshire to Luton – it was just unbelievable.

I know the lads that were in the visiting end, and they were all good lads. But they were totally outnumbered in there and it was a case of damage limitation on the day. Get them out, get them home safe, and the result's done. They'd gone in, they'd taken the piss – job done.

The other story was when we went to Leicester in about

1984. About five minutes from the end of the game we came out into the main road where their end is, and West Ham fans dived in the entrance where the rest of the Leicester fans were. It's gone right off, and we had to get a few more bodies on the ground because it was getting a bit grim. The gates were pushed open a little bit so we could all get in, and we had it as they were coming down the stairs. There was one old police officer there and he was stuck on his own. He was well in trouble, and I got beside him and helped him out because he'd got a right slap. He was an oldish lad, probably close to retirement age, and he was knackered. He was doing his job well, and, to be fair, he was a brave man, and I have a lot of time for brave people.

I said to him, 'Well, you face that lot,' which was our lot, 'and I'll face them.' And there were buckets being thrown at us – they were doing some work at the ground – there were ladders, and even the machine for painting white lines on the pitch. That weighed quite a bit and it was getting lobbed everywhere. There were Leicester and West Ham all fighting toe to toe at the bottom of the stairs. I had a straightener with a geezer and did him, and then the police came in and I got everyone moved away. Later I got a commendation from the police saying that I helped their officer in a dangerous situation and that it was a public-spirited action. But it didn't count for nothing later when I went to court, because the police didn't want that to be shown. They wouldn't let me use it, but I've still got it at home.

I thought Leicester were all right. It's another place where they always have a row and they're pretty game. But the last few times I've been up there when there's been a bit of trouble, I think they've been bullies. They've had pops at blokes with kids, and the respect I had for them has gone out the window.

WEST HAM v DERBY, CHARITY SHIELD, 1976

In 1976 Derby had a great side. They won the league when nobody gave them a chance. I think they pipped Liverpool in the last game of the season. And they were a fantastic team. Kevin Hector on the wing, Durban was playing for them and O'Hare. Boulton was in goal, but they had some quality players. A very good Derby team. The Charity Shield winners against the division one winners at that time. It was a lovely sunny day as normal at Wembley but we lost 2–0. We came out of our end round to Wembley Way where the Derby were. At the bottom of the stairs there was some scaffolding and we ran up with the scaffold ladder and cleared a few of them out of the way. But there was one crazy Derby fan who we gave a hiding, and he still kept standing there. And he followed us. We walked down the road and went into London, and he still followed us. He only took the one hiding, but we let him follow and it got a bit unnerving after a while. We thought, What's this nutter doing? He just kept following us. I remember one of them threw a brick and I got a little scar at the bottom of my mouth. I was lucky it didn't take any teeth out.

But it wasn't just Derby that day. They had all the Midlands with them. We never went with anybody else. We never wanted to. Rangers go with Chelsea, and this mob goes with that mob. We only ever went on our own. Saying that, I've got a lot of real good mates over at Queens Park Rangers. And I've always got a lot of time for QPR fans. I know they've not got the biggest mob in the world, but some of those boys are quality. Especially Jon-Jon, Wraithy and all their lot. Wraithy is like a son to me.

But Derby always put up stiff resistance. They were good opponents in those days with a bloody good football team.

WEST HAM v MILLWALL, 1978

The atmosphere between West Ham and Millwall fans has always been pure hatred. They cannot stand us and we cannot stand them. I don't think it's so bad now. I think the atmosphere's been muted, and the police make sure that nothing goes on. It's a tourist spectacle. You get the pikeys over there shouting and bawling at you, but that's all it is. In those days the feeling was on the back of your neck. Their hatred of us was born out of jealousy because we were always the bigger club with more fans. They were life's sufferers. We had jobs; they had none. They had no success when we did. And they were jealous of us.

My uncle actually played for Millwall and he told me it was like that back when he was there. I've only ever spoken to one Millwall fan. I've got mates who support almost every single team. I'm godfather to a Tottenham supporter's girl, I've got mates who support Queens Park Rangers, mates who are Chelsea fans, and I've even got mates who are Man United fans. But I can't bring myself to like or talk to any Millwall. The one exception is a bloke called Micky Daniels, who's one of the old firm over there. He's one of the faces. He's a bit older than me, and we met on a site when I was working and we hit it off quite well. But he was old school and he hated the way they are over there now. This young lot ponce through life and would stab you as soon as look at you. The atmosphere used to stick up on the back of your neck. There were no real arguments between the fans as such, it was just a feeling that you didn't like them and you wanted to hurt them. I don't hate anyone on this earth, but that lot I've just got no time for. And they've never changed.

We played them at home in the league in 1978 and they brought 800 fans and had one of the biggest police escorts back to the station that I've ever seen. They had helicopters, loads of horses in front and vans. They kept them in for ages afterwards. There were no scarfers in the 800 that day; it was all firm.

There's always a nasty atmosphere with any derby played, but not like this one. It's hard to describe. It's like your little brother is in a pram in a shopping centre and some scrote comes and nicks his toys. And all you want to do is get hold of him. It's the hatred that you feel if somebody has hurt your family. I've never felt that towards anyone other than them. It's something that is born in you and dies with you. They know me more than enough over there and they know that I hate them. And that's all I know. That, and the fact we beat them 3–0. I think Pop Robson got a hat-trick that day.

They cleared all the roads after the game and gave them this massive escort to the station. I was on the other platform to go home when they all came down. I was standing on the platform with a lad called Steve Lowly and a lad called Kevin Hatch, and when they recognised me they started throwing pennies. Plus the usual shouting and bawling that goes across. Then Tiny came up the front and said, 'Gardner, I'm going to do you.'

I said, 'Right, let's go up the top of the stairs, and let's have it now.'

He didn't want to move. I stood there, the train was coming and they all got on it. They pulled the tube doors apart a bit so that they could talk and spit at me. We got a banter going on between us, but I never got the feeling that he wanted to get off the train. His mates were going, 'Don't, Tiny, don't get off,' and they were holding him, but he was making no attempt to get off the train anyway.

I don't think he ever wanted to fight me. He had a good reputation and 800 of his mates, while I was with two others. I think, if you're going to have a go at somebody, that's the ideal time. I don't know if he didn't think he could win, or if he thought he could. I never thought I could lose. I never felt in those days that he really put himself out to find me because, if he did, he would have found me. I was always there. I was always at the front. I never hid.

MILLWALL 1980s

We were waiting at King's Cross Station in the morning before we went to a game, and three of them came in and were game as fuck. They were giving it large and everyone went out to have a pop at them. They had come to us and given it a right load of front. I remember one of them talking to me by name. They sort of drew us out into the road, and, before we knew it, it was an ambush and we were overtaken. There were loads of them around us, absolutely loads of them. We had some numbers ourselves that day and we were confident. These three geezers kept getting a slap and kept dragging everyone down to the road.

When they came out of St Pancras Station there were just loads of them. I remember one of the lads I was with said jokingly to me that he ran up the road and he passed a car and noticed it was doing 60 on the clock. I thought that was funny because it just about summed up the day. We could have come well unstuck on that day. It was a good victory to Millwall that day. Fair play to them. Victory where it's deserved.

But let's talk about Paul Dorset getting stabbed. Paul Dorset and his West Ham mates were going to Villa, who we were playing that day. They were on an underground train and a load of Millwall got on. Paul got stabbed in the heart and it was touch and go whether or not he would live. The word got through when we got to Villa that one West Ham had got stabbed, and I found out it was Paul. I was very angry, as he was a good mate of mine. Millwall were playing Huddersfield that day I believe. They would be coming in at King's Cross. The game went to the back of our minds. Everyone wanted to get Millwall that night; everyone was up for it. The talk was just about getting back and getting them in any way, shape or form we could. I was with Carlton Leach, Johnny Butler and all Paul's close mates. They were good mates of mine at that time too. It was very quiet on the train back.

It was the same sort of thing as Newcastle in 1981, when people wanted to get up there and get revenge for what they'd done. You could feel the tension. Everyone was really up for it. I don't think anything would have stopped us that night. I was just angry because Paul was a mate of mine and he'd been stabbed by the bully boys. I just knew we had to get down there and get them. This couldn't happen. Everyone was single-minded that night. You had to be. When you play Millwall you have to be single-minded to survive.

When the train pulled into London we already knew what time they would be coming back. Somebody had already sussed that out. We knew how long it took to get to the station, and as soon as we got there their train pulled in. The people I was with just walked through the middle of them. They weren't expecting it. If you do things like that, then people don't expect it. Just walk in like a normal person. I don't know how many were with us, but not many got through the police lines. We just walked straight up the platform where they were coming in, and when they got to the station we just steamed into them. Some of them turned and ran. Then the Old Bill came and pushed us out. In those days they never arrested you, because it took a man off the street. So they just tried to keep you apart, because, if there's 300 on each side, they need 600 police to arrest you all. So you knew that once you had got away with it you'd be all right. But that was naughty; that should never have happened.

I remember when they came off the station Millwall – unusually for them – just weren't up for it. I think they knew the severity of what had happened and they knew we wouldn't stand for it. They weren't surprised to see us, but the ones I saw at the front were shitting themselves. They really were. They didn't know what was gonna face them when they got off that train. It was a very brief exchange – it went on for seconds rather than minutes – and then the police were there. But I think the police were as pissed off about what had happened as we were.

The police eventually pushed us back and then got them all out and stood them alongside this wall. I don't know why, but I think they were trying to get them on to buses. I remember one of them came the other side of me and gave me a whack, which wasn't very brave of him. I chased him up the road and he didn't want to stop and go face to face. A lot of people were all right when it came to a group row or handbags at 50 paces, but when it came to standing toe to toe then that sorted out the men from the boys.

What set us out from the rest was that we'd have a row with somebody, we'd beat them, and it would all be over. But that lot would want to stamp on your head till your eyes were bleeding. We've never been like that. We've always shown a bit of chivalry, a bit of honour, a bit of courage. That's something they'll never have. People may question whether we show honour. But it is honour when your friend's getting hurt on the floor and you're fronted by five or six people, but you don't run off. You think of him and you pick him up. That's honour. Courage is to stand when you're confronted by a lot of people and you're surrounded. And chivalry is when you're outnumbered five to one and you go into them on your own. That's that. So, if anyone talks to me about values, I'll tell them no one had higher values than we had between us. I've never left a West Ham man down. When I worked in the clubs I never let the doorman down, and I've never let a West Ham fan down.

LEEDS v WEST HAM, 1981/82

We walked down to Elland Road from the station, which is quite a fair walk. There was loads of bother all the way down the road. Leeds is one of those places where they're real northerners. My version of a northerner may be a bit of a stereotype, but he's a pissed-up bloke in a pub. He can hardly see the game, let alone make a conversation about it. And anything that comes from five miles outside Leeds is soft to him. That's his whole attitude towards life: it's all about whippet racing and getting pissed up down the working men's club.

We were attacked nearly all the way down the road. All the usual ones who used to go with me were there. Leeds came at us all the time. They attacked us at regular intervals all the way to the ground, but we held our own. We got to the ground, and the police said, 'We're not going to let you in.' Then they decided they wanted to put us in this little corner bit which was terrible. You couldn't see anything. If there were any more of us in there we'd have been squashed to bits.

And I said, 'No, I'm not going in there. We want to go in the seats.'

He was a high-ranking copper and saw us as a mob and he said, 'You'll go where you're told.'

I said, 'No, we won't, we'll go home. If you don't give us a seat, we'll go home.'

He said, 'What do you mean?'

I said, 'Watch us. Come on, let's go home,' and 300 or 400 of us turned round and started walking.

He said, 'Hold on, what do you mean?'

I said, 'We've got the right to buy a seat. We want to buy a seat.'

After getting on his phone he decided to open this turnstile up and put us in South Stand seats. So we all went in and sat in the seats. They were scowling at us because we were prepared to go home. I wouldn't let him talk to me like I was a lump of shit. I've got my rights as a human being. If I want to sit, I'll sit. If I want to stand, I'll stand. I don't conform to anyone's standards. My missus says, if somebody says to me something's black, I'll say it's blue. I can't help it; it's in me. But I wasn't going to be told by this bloke what I could and couldn't do. I'd done nothing wrong. But he shouldn't have spoken to me like that just because I was a football fan. In those days they talked to you like you were a lump of shit. And I wasn't having it.

SOUTHAMPTON v WEST HAM, c 1984

Southampton's never a happy hunting ground for us. People sniff at Southampton, but to be fair they're not bad. They had a fair mob in there. About 20 of us got into Southampton's end and all of a sudden I looked round and we were surrounded by what must have been Southampton's top mob. This bloke who stood behind me was an absolute giant. He must have been seven foot tall. McGrath, Chris, Cliff, Ted and Vaughny were all in there with me. And I remember this giant of a man stood behind me with a black vest on. This fella had muscles on muscles. He was enormous. And we stood there and we kept hearing them say what they were going to do and what they weren't going to do.

At the end of the game, as soon as the final whistle went, I stuck it on him and he ran like a little baby. I couldn't believe this giant was running down the road. I was highly delighted to be truthful, because I thought he would be stiff resistance. But I stuck it on him and he literally ran like a rabbit down the road with his mates and I was kicking him up the arse. Anyone who was in there will tell you what an enormous man he was. He was bigger than the giant they call Mr Southampton. But, like most bodybuilders, they like doing the weights and that, but they don't like getting hurt. They don't like the old scars on their body.

NOTTINGHAM FOREST v WEST HAM, 1984/85

I was at a game at Forest with my current girlfriend Sarah. We were coming back over the bridge after the game and there didn't seem to be any threat of trouble. But all of a sudden we found that a load of Forest fans were on our left-hand side, giving it large. They started throwing a load of things at us, and a couple of lads got hit with bricks and went down. I managed to get my girlfriend up by the wall and my good friend Knobe, who is disabled, stood in front of her. He had withered arms, but he was as game as they come. And, if you've ever heard about Babsy at Chelsea with his disability, nothing could compare with Paul Knobe. He had the heart of a lion. I don't know if he's even still alive, but he had my utmost respect and he stood in front of Sarah as we fronted them. If we hadn't fronted them, they might have come over the road and we would have been in trouble.

So we walked towards them and they kept throwing things but we just kept on walking. In the end they shit themselves and ran off. They wanted to know, but they thought they were picking on 15 blokes with a girl. They couldn't have picked on a worse firm that day. There's a little estate just by the roundabout that's quite notorious. We always used to stop there because there was a nice chip shop, and sometimes we'd walk through the estate to get to the ground. But this particular day we were walking along the main road, and as we walked up towards the station after that fracas a Forest fan hit me from behind. I think he thought he was going to put me down, but he didn't, and when I just laughed at him I think he shit himself. But I wasn't one for chasing him down the road.

When we eventually got to the bus station all hell broke loose. It was going right off. There were railings all around the road like you have at some of these places, and they outnumbered us by 10 or 20 to one. These Forest, they were all the same little firm of Forest. They know you're not going nowhere, just seen that already back there, so they come up with a few more of them on a bit of a face-saving exercise. But I said to the lads, 'Don't go mad. Don't go jumping over the barrier to have a go at them; wait till a few of them come over the barrier and whack them. Then the other ones behind might not fancy it so much.' So that's what we did. We hung on until eight or nine of them got over the barrier and then we whacked them and the others ran off. If we'd gone over, we would have got done because we were outnumbered. If you cut off the head, the body will fall, and that's how it was that day.

GOOD AFTERNOON, GENTLEMEN, THE NAME'S BILL GARDNER

MAN UNITED v WEST HAM, 1980s

Manchester's never an easy place to go and we've had a few sorties at United. I don't like them, but I always used to look forward to their games, and we had some great battles coming out of the away end over the years.

The last time I was involved I got caught on the bridge that leads you up towards the road. There were only about 50 West Ham there, and all their mob were opposite. All the West Ham supporters were up by the wall, and I was in the middle of the road on my own. But their lot wouldn't come into me. They were all giving me, 'Oh where's your boys now, Bill?' And they were laughing at the lads because they were all pinned to the wall.

But I said, 'Don't worry about that, I'm here if you want it,' but they didn't want to know. I think that they had a bit of respect for me because I was on my own and I certainly wasn't up against the wall that day.

Then there was the time when I'd broken my leg. It was at Upton Park and I was with Paul Gane, Danny and Wraithy. I was just walking back to the car with my girlfriend Sarah, and a group of Man United supporters recognised me and fronted me out. They know me, Man United, they've known me for years, I was on crutches and they thought that I wouldn't respond to what they said. But they were wrong, because I didn't give a shit if I had one leg, no legs or five legs. Nobody talks to me like that. They were quite shocked, and I think they shit themselves to be truthful.

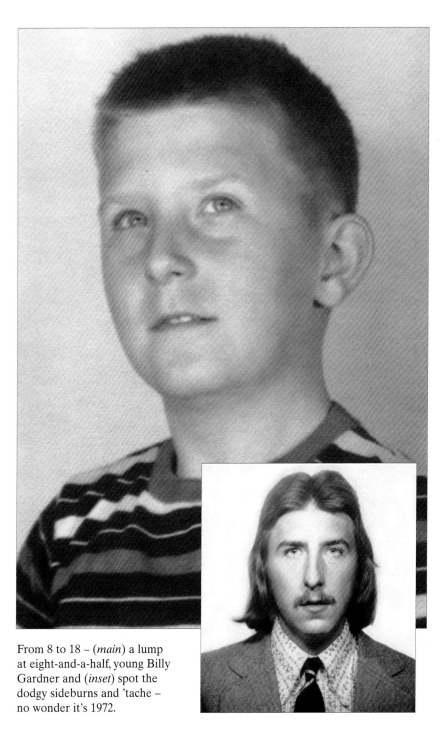

From 8 to 18 – (*main*) a lump at eight-and-a-half, young Billy Gardner and (*inset*) spot the dodgy sideburns and 'tache – no wonder it's 1972.

Top left and right: Uncle Bill in 1927 – could he have been an influence?

Bottom: William and Lottie in 1940, otherwise known as Mr and Mrs Gardner.

Top: My mother and me in happier times.

Bottom: Not yet, lads. Uncle Frank tends the grave.

Now it's Dr Bill Doolittle! *Top left:* He never won much, but I still looked after him.

Top right: With Bonzo.

Bottom: Pets Geordie and mummy pussycat (don't ask).

Top left: Meeting Ludo in an Italian airport.

Top right: Me with Harry boy.

Bottom: Round one! With champion boxer Steve Roberts – he's a Hammer.

The boys as they were.

Top left: This lot's been going for years.

Top right: In Ghent for pre-season with the Harrises Chris and Joe, plus Stanford.

Middle: There's some good boys here.

Right: I broke my wrist – just to go to Tiblisi.

The boys these days.

Top: Left to right Carlos, Ted, Bill, Ray 'Curly' Haimowitz, Simmo, Schobie, Bunter, Clivey Saul, Lol Schofield, Dick Scratcher.

Middle left: Swallow, Holloway and Cass at my party.

Middle right: A pre-season tour of Jersey.

Bottom: Friends Neil Duggan and the Waddell brothers – Steve and John.

Top left: All aboard, then!

Top right: Reunited back over the Hammers, after the ban was lifted.

Bottom: Ian Johnson (Spurs fan).

WEST HAM v MILLWALL, 2003

It had been put about on websites that Millwall were coming over to destroy the statue of our 1966 World Cup heroes. And I said to some people, 'Well, what are we going to do about it?' You just can't let them do that. So we came over on the Friday night and kept our eye on it. I said to the lads, 'Let's get it right. I retired in 1983, but you can't let people come and take liberties with the statue. You can't have it. I'll come over there. Anyone else coming?' Loads of them said, 'Yeah, we'll look after it.' I got over there about nine on the Friday night and parked up 10 yards from it, and I sat there and waited. No one came. Then it was 10.00 and 11.00 and still no one turned up. I waited till two in the morning and went home to the ridicule of my missus when I got indoors.

I guess I was a bit of a lone ranger on the statue, and the next morning the workmen boarded it up. And that's what they've done every time we've played them since. Even though I retired more than 20 years ago I still turn out every time we play Millwall because I just can't stand them.

CHAPTER THREE

OVER LAND AND SEA

WEST HAM v EINTRACHT FRANKFURT, 1975

We played Eintracht Frankfurt in the Cup Winners' Cup in 1975. We lost 2–1 in the first leg and Graham Paddon scored a great goal. Their ground was in the middle of a great big park, with a zoo round it and loads of amenities. You walked through these park gates and you ended up in the ground. We were queuing up to get a burger in this park when these Turkish geezers just pushed to the front of the queue. At that time I was with Carlos, who used to have a kebab shop down Mare Street in Hackney, and he's been one of my long-term mates. He said something in Turkish about them pushing in, and one of them pulled a knife out on us. Well, all hell broke loose. The circle went out like it always did. And all I can remember is that Carlos was fighting with this Turkish bloke as if it was the Marquis of Queensbury rules. It was unbelievable the way he was taking the piss out of the bloke. He had his arms up like an old prize-fighter, jabbing and moving, jabbing and moving.

Somebody passed me a piece of wood, so there I was, facing this bloke with a great big knife, humping this lump of four by two. He came at me once or twice and missed, and I missed him with the wood. And then he just turned and ran with his mates and we chased them out of the park. Carlos that night was unbelievable, and I just couldn't keep a straight face because I found it so funny. I don't know if it's a common thing for Turkish lads to carry a blade, but it must have been eight or nine inches long.

We went through in the second leg and it must have been one of the best atmospheres ever at West Ham. Night games at West Ham are unique. Things have changed since the all-seater stadium came in, and the hierarchy at West Ham keep on about people sitting down all the time. They just want you to be a cabbage: to sit there, clap politely, go home quietly and have no feelings or passion for the club. I think it's the same wherever you go, whatever team you support. They don't want the passion, and without that there's no point in going to football. I know we've had a crap team, but we've still been passionate about them. I find it hard now – you get there and nobody seems to want to get behind the lads like they used to all them years ago. In those days we only ever had football and that was it. There were no computer games or binge drinking.

In fact, that's another myth about us fans. All the research that has been done at, say, Leicester University about football hooligans and the tribal side of it is a right load of bollocks. I know for a fact that 90 per cent of the people I used to go with didn't even drink. And three-quarters of them never took drugs. So when they say it's all drink and drug related, it certainly wasn't with us. Sure, you might get the odd loudmouth who gets drunk, shoots his mouth off and gets arrested by the police. But the real hardcore lads didn't need a drink. What's the point in drinking? Anyone who ever had a row should know. When you drink you're only half the man you were when you were sober. My money's always on a man who's sober against a man who's drunk. The drunk man comes at you at 100 miles an hour, but his energy doesn't last. As long as you can withstand the first onslaught, you're the winner. It's as simple as that. Drink and fighting don't mix.

WEST HAM v ANDERLECHT, 1976

West Ham played Anderlecht in the Heysel Stadium, Brussels, in the Cup Winners' Cup final in May 1976. We'd had a fantastic night at Upton Park when we played Frankfurt in the semis and Keith Robson scored a cracking winner to put us through 4–3 on aggregate. That night was only ever beaten, I think, by the Ipswich play-off semi-final in 2004. The atmosphere was fantastic. The place was rocking, it was the greatest atmosphere I can ever remember at a football ground. Obviously we were all ready for the final. For many it was the first European trip they'd ever made following West Ham.

I was at home with my mum at the time in Hornchurch. I'd just met my second missus, Janice, and we went to the final with Paul Borontti and his wife Debbie and several other people like Peter Foley and Ted. They estimated that there were 15,000 West Ham fans, but I reckon it could have been 25,000. The end of the ground where we were had half the East End in it. We stayed in a hotel in the centre of Brussels and had some good nights out and went to their equivalent of Chessington World of Adventures. I bought a pair of bright-blue Adidas trainers and everyone slaughtered me for wearing the fucking things. The lads only seemed to wear black trainers back then, but later it became quite a popular colour.

I remember at the end of the ground there was loads of dust. Each time West Ham scored everyone jumped up and down and got covered in this dust. In the end we were soundly beaten by a good team, but it was still a fantastic experience. It was always my dream, even in the early days, to watch West Ham play in a European competition. I couldn't go when West Ham won it in 1965 because I didn't have the money. My dad actually went to the final but he only had the one ticket and I was a bit young for it at that time.

We also visited Brussels' red-light area – funny how any football fan will always head there. Certain lads went into the brothels and we went into a nice little Irish bar where they made us really welcome. Schobie did his trick where he hits himself with a metal tray – it has got to be seen to be believed. It's one of the funniest things I've ever experienced in my life. I laughed so much I cried. He sang the song 'Mule Train', and every time a certain bit came he hit himself on the head with the tray. The tray bent right across his head. Schobie is a real larger-than-life character. If he could have handled performing on the stage in front of a lot of people, he would have been one of Britain's best ever comedians.

But the night of the game the Brussels police were a little bit heavy-handed. I've always found that with these tin-pot countries. It's the only little bit of excitement they get, and I wouldn't say that Brussels is the most exciting city in the world. Their police were a little bit over the top as usual. There was a lot of trouble there, but there were police cars and sirens going all the time.

WEST HAM v CASTILLA, 1980

We played Real Madrid's nursery team, Castilla, and there was a lot of dispute over the seating arrangements as they had double-sold the seats. We went to the seats that were allocated to us and some Spanish blokes came in and said the seats were theirs. Then there was a bit of a fracas. Somebody said that some West Ham fans were pissing over the balcony on to the Spanish fans below. I personally didn't see this, but I heard from other people that this did happen. The police took a really dim view of it and came in with their rifle butts. I saw a little girl of about eight sitting with her mum and dad get hit with a rifle butt. I was with Schobie and little Joey who comes from Faversham. He was only a young lad then and he was really shitting himself. Me and Schobie got either side of him, and I was holding his head, just waiting for the wallop of a butt to hit us, but it didn't. We were pretty lucky.

We came out of the ground and the police were beating their batons like the Zulus in the film *Zulu*. Then I heard that this young lad had got run over by a coach driver that had mounted the pavement. This angered the West Ham fans quite a lot and needless to say there was quite a lot of trouble afterwards. When one of your own gets hurt, you respond in a very aggressive manner. I didn't actually know the lad personally, I must admit that, but he was a West Ham fan and nobody, no matter who you support, deserves to die in that manner. Retribution was had that night.

When we returned it was to the newspapers calling us scum and God knows what else, but they didn't realise what had happened. The Spanish police were having open season on us, and we managed to get hold of some tables from a bar to use as stretchers. The bloke in the bar was a good old boy, and he gave us beer mats so we could wipe the baton marks and the blood stains from the people that had got hurt.

West Ham's commercial manager at the time went out in one of the hired coaches to try to pick up the stragglers, because every West Ham fan that was on his own was getting picked off by the police. They were just jumping out of vans, beating you up and driving off to find their next victims. So he went out in a coach, and fair play to him for that. He knew that on the night we were not to blame for anything that went on.

But when we came back we got absolutely slaughtered by the English press. Some of the boys wanted to put a wreath on the pitch out of respect for the lad that died. West Ham's club officials at the time refused. I was approached by the assistant commercial manager Dennis Smith, who told me he knew there was going to be a lot of trouble that day and he didn't want this wreath to be put on the pitch. I told him that, if it wasn't put on the pitch, there'd be even more trouble. In the end they backed down, and what we did was the least you should expect when somebody dies in those circumstances. But the West Ham hierarchy wouldn't admit that the fans were picked on that day.

Billy Bonds was quoted in the papers saying the fans were scum, but I approached him when he was sitting in his car at the ground and he told me he'd never said it. I also approached John Lyle and he told me he hadn't said it, but somebody did. Somebody said we were all animals, but you try telling that to the father of a little eight-year-old girl who's been rifle-butted. He'll tell you a different story. So will the boys we patched up on top of the tables in the bars – that night was the nearest I've ever been to being a surgeon. Mind you, I have stitched up a few people in their senses.

WEST HAM v TIMISOARA, 1980

In Romania in the 1980s you could only get chicken and chips to eat. Chicken and chips was on the menu six times. But it was very poor at that time and nobody had much over there. It was even poorer than Russia, where we went later in the year. It was a common sight when you went down the road to see a woman digging the road up with a drill, with a fag in the corner of her mouth.

I remember I shared a room with Dennis Lepine one time, and when I woke up in the morning my mouth was like a Chinese wrestler's jockstrap and I wanted to get a drink. I thought I'd go for a walk around because I've always been an early riser, and it was still dark when I got up. And what I always remember about Romania was nobody spoke to each other. They all went to work but nobody spoke to each other. You saw people with their heads down and grey faces. The bus was an old truck that had been converted with seats in it. I remember seeing this queue for a bakery, and people were just pointing to what they wanted. So I pointed to some rolls and what I thought was a bottle of milk. She took the lid off and gave it to me and I went over into the corner to drink it. Everyone looked at me and I discovered it wasn't milk, but natural yoghurt. In those days natural yogurt wasn't thought of as the healthy food that it is now. I remember them looking at me thinking what a fucking idiot this bloke was. I took it back to our room and put it on the side for Dennis, and he did exactly the same. So the food was crap, but it was a great trip.

We played Politecnica Timisoara in the 1980 Cup Winners' Cup. I remember I met a couple of Romanians and was chatting away outside the hotel when a car pulled up. These KGB or whatever got out, gave one of these guys a slap, threatened me with a gun and said if I got involved they would shoot me. Then they gave him another slap, got back in the car and drove off again. He got up and I said, 'What's that about?'

He said, 'It happens all the time. They thought I was trying to deal with you on the black market.'

I got his name and address and sent him over some things when I got home. I never heard from him again, but he had told me they would look through every parcel that was sent. Even books that were sent used to have lines blanked out if they didn't want people to read them. Everything was vetted. It was a grim country. I've been twice and that's twice too many.

All they wanted to do was touch you all the time. They'd never seen English people before in this particular part of Romania and they just kept touching you. I remember Schobie got the right hump because one of them kept touching him. I think he stuck it on the bloke. Before we knew it he'd got all his pals there and then all of a sudden the water cannon's come in and they've aimed it at this lot and that was the end of that. They didn't use it – they only had to aim it at them. But they took us to the pitch and took us through the changing-room area where the players were getting changed. It was a pretty grim place.

When we played Steava Bucharest in 1999, 12 out of a party of 30 got pickpocketed at some stage or another. They're a terrible race of people, but then again it's one of those places where you need to see how they live. Then you understand why they're all over here now.

WEST HAM v DYNAMO TBILISI, 1981

West Ham played Dynamo Tbilisi over two legs in the 1981 Cup Winners' Cup. We got beaten 4–1 at home by probably the best side that West Ham have ever played. They totally murdered us. They were a pleasure to watch and they got a standing ovation at the end. I was asked by my friend Mike Ross to get some West Ham people together to go over there on a trip. He said he'd let me go for nothing if I got some bodies, which I did.

At the time I was working for the council and they said I'd used up all my holiday entitlement and if they allowed me the time off to go they'd have to do it for everyone else. But I was desperate to go, so I decided to whack my wrist with a hammer. It was entirely my own decision and I took six paracetamol tablets as I was determined to get the week off. The first blow didn't hurt, so I tried again. That hurt more than the first and it started to swell immediately. I went straight up to the hospital because I'd heard a cracking. I was still a bit shocked when they said I'd broken it in six places. So I got the certificate I needed for the week and had my arm in plaster right up to my elbow. This brainwave eventually cost me 27 weeks off work and

I still keep the plaster cast at home to this day as it's covered in players' signatures obtained when we had to check in and out of the airports.

We flew to Moscow, which was under nine inches of snow when we got there, and then we went from there to Tbilisi where, believe it or not, it was 23 degrees centigrade. We spent a day or two in Moscow, and Mike Ross booked us into the same hotel as the players, but the West Ham commercial manager kicked up a fuss so we had to move. But we did manage to go to the same bar that they were in that night. We had a marvellous time in Moscow. Anyone who goes there should check out the subway – it's got glass chandeliers and holes cut out of the wall for people to shelter in if there's a nuclear explosion. There are big cabinets filled with tinned food so they can survive a blast – it was a real education.

We went to Red Square and saw people queuing up to see Lenin's tomb, and it was great to be there at a time when Russia wasn't really a place that people went to. It was an amazing thing to go to department stores where they sold the same things on every floor. Every floor sold bits. If you wanted to make your own radio, you could get bits there all day long. If you wanted food, you really struggled. I was with a bloke called Steve Bean in one of the department stores and we watched them bringing in carpets with armed guards, and there were women fighting each other to get a proper carpet.

We flew from Moscow down to Tbilisi, and when we

travelled from the hotel to the ground the streets were lined with people and soldiers who immediately stopped and saluted us. The ground could fit 80,000 people and there were only 300 of us. They left a little area open for us to sit in, and as we came into the ground all 80,000 people got up and clapped. They had a big banner along the side saying, 'Welcome to the sportsmen of England.' It sticks in my memory to this day. It was a bad feeling to be thrashed so severely in the first game, but it was worth the journey and we won the second leg 1–0. Stuart Pearson scored the goal in the final minutes.

We had a great time with the black market because the Russians do like a deal. It was no good going to the bureau de change to get your money. You waited for a knock on your door where they'd give you four to six times the rate for your pound note. You could also sell everything you had. Any sports gear, anything like Adidas or Slazenger, or chewing gum, cassettes, English music – they loved it. I think it worked out that I came back with 40 quid more than I went out with. So a good time was had by all.

But once again the attitude of the West Ham hierarchy towards the fans wasn't what it should have been. There was always this 'us and them' attitude that goes on to this day. They'll never know how lucky they are that they've got 30,000-odd fans that will follow them through thick and thin. The Board of Directors have got about as much ambition as a prisoner on death row.

There was all this nonsense prior to the flight to

Moscow, when they tried to get us out of the plane that the club's officials were on. But we had booked the plane seats through the proper channels, so they couldn't shift us and they had to put up with a no-man's land with two or three rows of empty seats between them and us. I was up to date on what was going on the whole time because Mike Ross was keeping me informed, but the then commercial manager was a right arsehole. He's a man that I despise immensely. And all I can say is good riddance to him. He really did resent that I was there. It's a shame because the first time I met him I saved him and his son from getting a good hiding up at Barnsley. West Ham put Mike Ross under a lot of pressure because they wanted the plane we had booked first for themselves, but he fought his corner well. He was actually a Liverpool fan living in London. We won the day and we were allowed to go.

We stayed in this massive hotel in Tbilisi and I had a knock on the door because I was the courier. It was the owner of the hotel saying I'd better come with him because there was trouble upstairs. I was on the ground floor at the time, and all of a sudden I heard a bang and looked out of the window and a settee just missed my head by about three feet. It looked like somebody was lobbing things out of the top window. When we went up to the room the people who were staying there had completely stripped it. The heater had been ripped off the wall, the settees had been thrown out the window, the bed was gone – everything had gone. I didn't agree with this because it was wanton damage, but the thing that made me laugh was when I went in the toilet. One of them had shit in the bath and put a Union Jack in it, and this Richard was floating up and down the bath tub with a flag in it. Hard as I tried not to laugh and to be the responsible adult I was supposed to be, I just couldn't help it. It was like one of these little toys kids have with an outboard motor that goes up and down the bath.

They found out whose room it was and the police came and arrested them. The only way they would let them out was if the damage was paid for. Everyone put money into the whip to get the fellers out and they returned home. I was a bit pissed off because I had taken responsibility to marshal the group, and I wanted it to go smoothly because I wanted more work from the bloke. It's nice to go to football and get paid for what you love doing. There was no reason for the room to be trashed like that. But I don't care what you are, you could be a lay preacher, if you'd seen that Richard in the bath, you couldn't help but find it funny. I didn't want to show my laughter in front of the bloke, but in the end I just couldn't help it.

WORLD CUP, SPAIN, 1982

England games are sometimes open season for other countries' police to have a go at our people. They know that with the England fans' reputation they can do anything, and our country will not back anyone up. They use us for practice. And nobody in this country has the bollocks to stand up and say, 'Hold on a minute. These are our people. Why are kids coming home with rifle-butt marks or pistol whips across their heads? Why have people got hit with batons when they're not involved in anything?' But unfortunately that's not the way the world is. The world is now a place where nobody would piss on you if you were on fire. Women can get raped in London, but people turn away because it's not their problem. If a pensioner gets her money nicked, people think it's not their problem either. But I'm afraid it is my problem – and I'll make it my problem as long as I have breath in me.

In 1982 I was asked by Mike Ross to take a coach load of fans to the 1982 World Cup in Spain. It was a chance to take in some football and have an earner at the same time. The travel company was hiring me as added insurance – using me as some sort of security chaperone. I think he'd seen what my presence could do when we'd previously travelled in the Cup Winners' Cup to watch West Ham. England's first group games were based in Bilbao, and we were to stay in a little village halfway between Bilbao and San Sebastian called Zarautz.

I met the coach at Knightsbridge and it consisted mostly of Chelsea, Southampton, Tottenham and Man United supporters. It was a good mixture, and although I didn't know any of them I could tell it was a coach load of seasoned England campaigners. There was that Rule Britannia attitude among them and a lot of the Chelsea lads had their heads done in the England flag. The travel company had asked me to make sure that everyone behaved, but that they enjoyed themselves too. I immediately told them the score with me and that if anyone was late at any of the pick-up points they would be left behind. I don't wait for anybody. I think it's a weakness in a person if they can't be on time.

So we made our way from Knightsbridge to the ferry, and when we got to Calais two people didn't come down when they should have done to meet the coach. I gave them a couple of minutes, which is all I could do because the cars were leaving underneath, and we went without them. We travelled down to Zarautz, which took 24 hours, only stopping twice to go to the toilet. The coach was very uncomfortable. Not many people spoke to me through the journey, but we finally ended up in this very nice hotel, positioned on a beautiful sandy beach that went on for about half a mile. The area was one of those quiet little tourist places. We went in there and everything was going fine. We heard it was an Eta stronghold, but we didn't see any evidence of that.

After a few days there I got ill with food poisoning. I was resting in my hotel bedroom around eight in the evening and I heard shouting and what sounded like guns going off and bricks hitting the building. I rushed outside and up on to the roof, which was a big patio area where people could sit and relax. I realised the locals were throwing things at the hotel because a couple of the boys had draped their England flags over the balcony. I tried to stop them from throwing things and our lot from chucking them back, but to no avail. A missile went past my ear and that was it. I thought it was a case of self-preservation.

Two Tottenham fans were on the ground floor and I asked them, 'What have you got there to throw?' And they said they had some cans of lager in the fridge. So I said, 'Well, I'll have them.' So I had their 24 cans of lager. I started lobbing frozen cans of solid lager, using them like grenades to keep back the local hordes that were trying to invade our hotel. I twigged that there were some people behind the wall of some shops facing the hotel who seemed to be the main antagonisers. They were throwing and ducking back behind the wall. So I realised I could throw two cans one after the other in quick succession. If I missed with the first one, the second would cop him as he popped his head out. I caught one of them on the head with this can, and the last I saw his mates were dragging him away by his feet.

Throughout the chaos I will never forget the help of a Man United fan, who jumped down two floors to help me, injuring his ankle in the process, and a Chelsea fan, who steamed up from the lower floor. I've never known his name, but I know he came from Bookham in Surrey and was an electrician. He showed extreme bravery on the day to help me. After a little while, and several lots of garden furniture going over the top, it sort of calmed down.

Before then people had gone out in groups of four or six to explore or just find a bar, while some went out on their own. I went out on my own too. In the morning we'd usually go on the beach and have a few games of football against the locals. It went OK the first few days. A couple of heavy tackles went in, most of them by us, but it was nothing to do with us not liking them. It was a game of football, and we were there to win the game. That's an attitude perhaps our team could have a bit more often. I always find that the fans of clubs often want to win more than the teams do. It certainly seems to be the way at West Ham.

After the first couple of days you could sense a change and it became very aggressive. Suddenly we knew we were up against it. They made it known that they didn't like us. In shops their general attitude was that they didn't want us there and that we were scum. It was also clear they thought we shouldn't have won the Falklands conflict, which had just happened. I didn't hear so much of it from the supporters that were staying in Bilbao, but where we were was real banjo country, and they certainly backed the Argentineans 100 per cent. There were two from Argentina staying in town and one of them seemed to be pulling the strings. You've got to remember Argentina is Spanish speaking and that makes an easy bond.

I think everyone wanted to show a bit of patriotism, but it wasn't so much of a Falklands thing with us. Most people didn't know where the Falkland Islands even were because it was so far away. People related more to what was going on over in Ireland, and when you watched England they would sing 'no surrender to the IRA'. Anyway, you sensed there was plenty of anti-British feeling.

Some of the lads feared that there might be reprisals over what had gone on, and the following evening I was sitting on my own in a bar having a drink. One of the lads in the coach party came up and told me he'd been in a disco and had paid an old brass for sex but she'd taken his money and not come up with the goods. He asked me if I could do anything about it. So I went into the disco where he said this girl was and went down a set of stairs on to the dance floor. At the far end of the disco there were two brasses with two pimps sitting there. I later found out that the two pimps were these Argentinean nationals and they weren't too happy about the Falklands.

So I went down and said, 'Look, the geezer's paid the bird for sex, and she's not coming over with it. What do we do?' He just pointed up at the balcony of the building, and there were loads of people standing there with lumps of wood, baseball bats and God knows what else. I thought we were in deep shit. There were about four of us standing there at the time and I said to the boys, 'When I tell you, you make a bolt for the door.' We went for it, and one of the boys got hit with something and jumped on my back. I made my way up the stairs and dived through some big, open door-size window shutters. On the way out an iron bar or something caught me on the leg. It wasn't too serious, but it was enough to slow me up. The four of us managed to make our way back into the hotel which was just round the corner, but almost immediately there was a big horde of Spanish with these two Argentineans outside.

They were screaming and shouting at us and they wanted to get in. I just stood in front of the door and thought I'd better try to keep them out as I was in charge of this party. I think they were high on drugs because one of them was like a lunatic. He came right through the closed hotel front door – literally just charged through the glass panel of the door with a gun. My first reaction was that I had to put this bloke out of action before he killed somebody. He shot one bullet into the roof of the bar in the hotel and one just above the television that missed me by about three inches. I heard lumps coming off the glass chandelier, and it went dark because he'd shot the lights out. Nobody shouted. There was no screaming. It was pure shock, I think. The only noise you could hear was them screaming outside trying to get in. The English people who were in the bar at that time were cowering under their seats.

When the guy had run up the front stairs I thought I'd just block him, and I already had a metal bar-stool to hand. So when he started firing I just whacked him with it as hard as I could. I stuck the stool in his shoulder. He was walking around with it sticking out of his shoulder as if somebody was going to sit and have a ride on his back. He went out as quick as he could and fell down the stairs, and they carted him away. We beat the rest of them out and waited in the hotel. We just stood there in case they came back up again. I felt we were pretty lucky to survive somebody shooting at us. It really was a crazy moment and

I felt so on my own, like I've felt a lot of times in my life. I always felt when there was trouble that I was in a bubble and I stayed totally calm. Everyone who mixes with me will tell you that I'm calm and methodical and that I think about the situation. I sometimes feel that I can see what's going to happen a few seconds before it starts, and that's helped me in the past.

We were up against a community that didn't like us. The way in which they bombarded our hotel was fanatical and had nothing to do with football. It was because we were English. I think, if we hadn't made a stand, they would have walked all over us. About 30 of them hung on for a while outside and it all went quiet inside and outside the hotel. And then the police came and tried to move them away. There are two types of police in Spain – the brown shirts and the blue shirts. One seems to be the local lot and the other are like the heavy mob. The local ones came first and they didn't seem to have any priorities, and then the heavy mob came and started moving people away.

A few hours later the police came into the hotel wanting to know what went on. I told them I was the courier for this group and that these loons had come through the door and we'd taken action to stop them. Anyone who was hurt in that serious little conflict had to go to hospital and I went with them. I felt it was my duty and my job to look after these England fans, whether they were Southampton, Tottenham, Man United or Chelsea. Besides, some of those lads had really supported me and I had a lot of time for the

Man United lad who jumped two floors to help. And I would still like to know that Chelsea lad's name because he should have been a Hammer. And I hear all these people talk about England games, England fans this, England fans that. Sure England fans get pissed up, sure England fans are loud, that's the way we are as a race.

The owner of the hotel in Zarautz was quite a nice man, but he couldn't understand the English way of enjoying themselves. He was very quiet and we spoke at length about several things. But he told me he just couldn't work it out. He was moaning about the boozing and the noise. I tried to explain to him that these are English people on holiday and this is the way we are.

People don't understand it. I mean, I'm like most folk, I like the quieter way of life, but I understand what people do, it's simple. We're not like the Spanish people, we are not like the Italians, we are English people and that's the way we behave. They go over there, the fellas, for their holiday, they have a drink, they want to enjoy themselves.

The police are only too keen to get into them, give them a hiding, knowing full well that nobody back in this country will stick up for them and ask why the police do that. And that's what it's always going to be like when England play abroad. It's open season on us and people don't seem to realise that unless they've been there and know the score.

At the hospital one lad had to be stitched up, while a Chelsea fan and another one who had got a knock on the head needed treatment. After we'd got back to the hotel the police arrived again. This time they arrested everyone who had put their name down in the hospital, including myself, and we were banged up in the cells in Zarautz. I thought we might see our mad gunman loon as he wasn't at the hospital, and I wondered how he got treatment. They must have known he'd get charged, so they didn't take him to the hospital. I hurt him badly, but not as bad as he would have hurt us.

I tried asking the police why they hadn't nicked any of them and they'd only nicked us, but I didn't seem to be getting anywhere. Everyone was pretty pissed off. We thought we'd be stuck in there for a long while. So I asked to see the Ambassador. After a day the British Ambassador flew up from Madrid. He spoke to us and said because there was a shooting incident involved and with the Falklands in everyone's mind he didn't want to blow it out of all proportion. It was the only incident in the whole World Cup where guns were used, and the British Government wanted to play it down. They didn't want to know. They couldn't give a shit. That's the view I took when he said that none of us could say anything about what happened. He would get us all out if we didn't say anything to the press, which obviously we agreed to.

So we got let out, and I can tell you it was a relief to be free. We heard afterwards that some of the people that were involved were Eta. The place was an Eta stronghold and they all ran that way: Bilbao, Zarautz and San

Sebastian. It actually made the main headlines in a Spanish paper, and somebody who spoke English and Spanish translated the story and they described it exactly the way I have. As I say, it was the only incident where guns were used in the whole of the World Cup.

I didn't go to many England games. I went to watch England play Malta in a friendly a couple of years ago. And I went to Norway in 1982 when we got beaten and the Norwegian TV presenter made that famous outburst: 'Winston Churchill, Margaret Thatcher, we have given your boys a hell of a beating', but the England team isn't really my scene. I like to be around people I can trust, and I'm afraid that some of the northern fellers you met at these England games did like too many beers for me. So I don't go to them any more. I've never had the same feeling for England as I have for West Ham. I'm sure it might sound treasonous, but that's the way it is for me. And I've been told that I've watched West Ham play abroad more than any other fan in the club's history. So, if that is right, I'm pleased to hold that record.

WEST HAM v DEN HAAG, August 1986

We saw 'The Monster' when we went from Groningen to The Hague. There were four of us – Danny Gray, Sarah, me and someone else who I can't remember. There had been some trouble on the ferries and they'd stopped the West Ham supporters going. We were sitting in the stand and the away supporters bit was totally empty. And the Monster was below us. He was like a fucking big baby. The fucking Monster, my arse. His little firm were all about 13 and he must have been 30. He was a bit thick. He was one of these blokes who was born massive but didn't have too much upstairs. They were setting fires under the stand and they kept looking at the away bit, but we were right behind them looking at them. There was definitely something wrong with him. I remember when he was jumping up and down he was like a fucking idiot. If he had knocked around with us, we'd have said, 'Get the fuck out of it, you idiot.' A right doughnut.

We have met Den Haag a few times in games. There was a friendly that got pretty bad, because they were up for it. But the second time, in the Cup Winners' Cup, the boot was on the other foot, as we had a fair little firm there.

WEST HAM v NK OSIJEK, 1999

When we played Croatian side NK Osijek I travelled over there with John Waddell, Neil Duggan and a couple of other people. We flew to Zagreb and then went by train across country. I think it was four hours on the train to where we were playing in Osijek, which is right out of the way. We stayed in a hotel which had been previously bombed and the balcony had been blown off. It was a pretty tatty sort of hotel, but it was really nice, with a good atmosphere. We went out on the booze in the town centre and I remember it being a really nice sunny day. You could see the bullet holes in the walls, but people seemed to be very happy.

It really was too hot to be roaming around in the daytime, so everyone congregated around the main square, drinking all day. There were German West Ham supporters all over the place. Yeah, German West Ham supporters. We were talking and having a drink with them and we all went for a pizza. Everything went fine, and we got the result we deserved in the end.

So there we all were, drinking all day long and talking football, when a Channel Four representative approached me and said, 'Are you Bill Gardner?' I said, 'Yes,' and he said, 'We'd like you to present something on the pitch before the game, and they'll give a present back.' I said I would, and I wasn't that surprised by it all. I'm never shocked by anything now, but I was very honoured to be asked to represent the supporters. Like Bobby Moore said, it was always West Ham United, not just West Ham. And that's how we've always got to be in my eyes. The day we're not West Ham United any more, that's the day I pack it in.

The Croatian fans' main firm was called Kaharta, and they met us in the bar in the town centre by the square and we all sat together talking. And they gave us 20 blue shirts. I had two of them and we went back and got ready for the game. West Ham gave us a hat to swap with their supporters. Eddie Gillam, the kit manager, gave me that by the ground before the game because we had nothing to give them. I wanted to give them a pennant, but they gave me a baseball cap and I swapped it with the Croatian fans on the pitch just before kick-off. I didn't know it was going to be broadcast live on telly in England. There was a bit of a clap, but I don't think a lot of people knew what was going on. I shook hands with the lads, who were actually two of the doormen I'd been speaking to previously. Out on the pitch with me was a lad called Maskell who was a bit the worse for wear. Before the game we were taken inside the stadium, and Maskell went in the changing rooms and told the team that we'd come a long way, so they'd better win or else they'd be in trouble. He's a funny man. I just went and stood back on the terraces and watched the game, and West Ham won well. It was the first UEFA Cup match in West Ham's history.

That night we went into the town centre and I got talking to a doorman at one of the clubs, who was telling me how guns were freely available since the war. All the doormen had to carry one because somebody would just pull out a gun on them if they didn't let them in and they had to defend themselves. We sat outside talking and the police were opposite watching us and I got talking to one of them. I asked if there was anywhere open late, and he said there was a club down the road but it was too late to get a bus. But he asked me how many of us wanted to go and, when I said there were 60–100 of us, he said, 'All right,' and he called up all kinds of lorries, cars and vans and transported us up to the club in these police vehicles.

Maskell wouldn't get in the police car because he'd never been in one without being handcuffed. So they had to handcuff him to make him get in. The police came in with us, and it was quite a nice club apart from one of the locals got a bit funny with Jock. We think he was a bit gay, and Jock was going to whack him. But I told the policeman that this geezer was causing a problem and they slung him out. He said they didn't want to upset us. We had a really good night in the club. The thing that struck me the most about Croatia was how friendly the people were. They've got nothing, but they'd give you everything. I've got nothing but time for them. They are an expressive people who've got the values that I rate. I like Croatia and I think the people are great. I don't think I will ever forget being asked to represent the West Ham fans on the pitch in Osijek. It was one of the highlights of my life.

CHAPTER FOUR

ARREST, BREAKDOWN, TRIAL, THEN TRIUMPH

The day my eldest boy James was born, and he's now 21, was the day I packed it up, because I didn't want my son to grow up without parents at home to look after him. Not only that, but Sarah, who I've been with for 21 years, would never have put up with me doing what I did before I met her. So when all the crap happened it came completely out of the blue.

At six-thirty in the morning there was a knock on the door. I had a broken leg at the time and was on crutches. I went to the door and looked through the surveillance hole and saw a load of police officers standing outside. I opened the door and said, 'What's the problem?'

They said, 'We're arresting you for being the leader of the ICF, and we've got a search warrant.' They called me 'The General'.

I let them in and I sat down and I said nothing. They went through my place, tipping everything over like they normally do, and Sarah asked if they wanted tea and biscuits, which they all had. At the court hearing, they were asked how I was that morning, and the police said I was aggressive. They didn't mention that I offered them tea and biscuits. But another copper told them the truth when he gave his evidence, so that totally blew what they were trying to do out of the water.

So they searched the place till 8.45 in the morning and all they found were a few videos of games, like everybody has. There were no weapons at all because I was retired. They took me out and there was snow on the ground. They flanked the path to the van and I got in. They got a bit heavy with me in the van and I got a little bit heavy back. So we came to an agreement that it might be a good idea to have a nice quiet journey up the road rather than me waving my crutches at them. So we went to North Woolwich Police Station, where I was booked in, and they began the procedure of questioning me.

They then took me from North Woolwich up to East Ham Police Station, and when I was getting booked in the sergeant who arrested me went into the control room and I heard a massive round of applause. I took it that they were clapping him because he'd arrested me. I couldn't believe it, because I had a broken leg with a plaster cast on and it took eight of them to arrest me. They could have sent a policewoman on a bike and she could have done it. They put me in a cell with

Taffy, who was another they'd nicked and were holding at East Ham Police Station. I didn't understand why they had put us in together and immediately thought the cell must be bugged. They wanted us to talk about things, but as I wasn't involved in anything I had nothing to talk about. When they decided they weren't going to get anything from us, they took me out and put me in another cell.

In the meantime, Sarah had come up with my mate John Wraith and they told her I was at East Ham when they'd already moved me back to North Woolwich. They kept running her up and down the road like a yo-yo. And they questioned me for 11 hours. I answered every single question they put to me. I felt like I had nothing to worry about because I was innocent and that was it. I'm not denying what happened before 1983, and I know I'm no angel, but I'm also not a criminal. If I had the chance again I'd do exactly the same things. You have to have principles in life and I certainly do.

I was questioned, charged with conspiracy to cause affray and bailed to appear in court the next day, when I was refused bail and was taken by van to Brixton Prison. I spent eight days in the prison hospital because of the plaster cast. All the rest of the lads they'd arrested went on the wing, which I'd have preferred. During the interrogation they explained to me that it was serious. They said I was looking at 10 years. They were also giving the usual spiel about how I had a good-looking wife who wouldn't still be around for me in 10 years.

The first time I saw who was in the dock with me, it hit home to me that this must be really serious. Some of the people in the court I didn't even recognise. I knew Andy Swallow, Cass Pennant, Big Ted and Paul Dorset, but that was it. And I just kept faith that whatever they built against me might fall apart. They were trying to say that we sat down round tables and plotted violence at football matches. I'd never sat round a table with anyone who they put up in court. They mentioned the InterCity Firm, but I never really regarded myself as being part of that group. I always went on my own and I regarded the people that came with me as part of my group, not the ICF. But we all got labelled the same. They refused me bail and I just couldn't believe it. That came as a real blow, because my solicitor said I'd get it because I had a broken leg. But I was refused it and I was sent to Brixton.

It was the first time I'd ever been in prison. I was innocent so I was pretty apprehensive. When I got there I had a full body search, and in my hand I had a picture of my little boy James. You're not allowed to take anything in with you, and one prison officer said, 'Throw it in the bin.'

I said, 'I ain't throwing it in the fucking bin. You come and get it.'

But another one said to me, 'That's all right, put it down your plaster.'

So I had that, and I went into the cell in the hospital wing and met all the other people in there. Nobody's ever guilty in prison; everyone's innocent. But in this case I really was.

I applied for bail again after eight days and they set it at £32,500, which was more than a murderer was getting at that time. A lad who I hardly knew put up £20,000. His name was Lee Jones and he lived out at Ruislip before moving to Ireland. I have never found him to thank him and I've always wanted to. If he reads this I hope he takes it as a thank you for what he did for me that day. I hadn't known my girlfriend, Sarah, for long, but she and her family put up some money and so did my mum. So I got bail and was told there was going to be a committal hearing.

The press were everywhere. I had the local radio station camped in my garden with one of those big fluffy microphones hanging in the top window. It was like a giant caterpillar trying to get through the top window. The police used to empty the dustbins to try to find anything I might have been trying to get rid of. Obviously there was nothing. One day I caught them running out of the garden with a black bin bag and jumping into the back of a van.

Brixton was quite an interesting experience because I'd never been in prison before. Sarah came to visit me and it broke my heart to see my little boy having to come to see his dad in prison. I don't know what was going through his mind, as he was only small at the time. Sarah brought me in some milk, some Tizer and some apple juice and other bits and bobs, but because I was in the prison hospital wing I wasn't allowed the same foods as if I was on the main wing. You couldn't have Old Jamaica chocolate because they reckon you could make alcohol out of it. You couldn't have Duracell batteries because then you could make bombs. So at the end of the day it was a real learning curve.

They don't give you tins or bottles for obvious reasons, so they put all your drinks or food into a plastic container. And the screw took great delight in putting the milk in, then the apple juice and then the Tizer. You can image what it looked like all curdling together. He looked at me with a funny, vacant look, as if to say, 'Yeah, drink that, you idiot.' He had an equally vacant look when I hit him with my crutch, which drew great applause from the other inmates. Most of them were in there for the Brixton riots at the time, and all I could hear was people saying, 'Go on, Honky, give it to him,' which I did. All of a sudden I was surrounded by other screws, who pulled me to the floor and took me back to the cell.

I had a pillowcase in my mouth with stuff in it and I could hardly walk with it swinging from side to side hitting the crutches. It was quite heavy and I had it between my teeth like an animal holding on to its prey. All of a sudden some bloke's burst through and got hold of the bag and said, 'Here you are, mate, I'll carry that for you.' The screws let him carry it to where the hospital wing was and I noticed he had a yellow stripe down his trousers and he had an Irish accent. I went into the hospital wing of the prison and told a couple of the fellas in there, who were much more experienced than I was about what went on in there, and they told me who that he was one of the Irish bombers that hit the Horse Guards on The Mall, but he showed me a bit more kindness that day. He was supposed to be an animal, but it was the screws who showed no kindness towards another human being. All they wanted to do was make me feel like a lump of shit by carrying this thing in my mouth. And it was a hard pill to swallow.

On the Sunday someone had asked me if I was going to church. I thought it was strange, because I wouldn't have thought any of them would be churchgoers. I certainly wasn't one of the one per cent of the population who went to church. But this guy said, 'Come on, it gets us out for an hour or so.' So I went to the chapel and I was surprised to see so many people in there. Then I realised why. Because it was communion, you got a drink of wine, and that's what it was all about. And it was an amazing experience, like nothing I'd ever seen before.

But it was a hard time while I was in there, and I think I had a nervous breakdown because I was writing letters home saying things that just didn't sound like me. It was like somebody else. I was saying things like, 'When this is over we'll move somewhere, and we'll change our names.' Looking back I think I was really ill. It took me a long, long while to get over it. Things like that stay with you for ever. I'd had the shock of breaking my leg twice in one calendar year, my dad was dying, my mum was seriously ill, and here I was in prison facing serious charges and knowing I was innocent.

But I pulled myself together at the court case. I knew that I had been going through a rocky moment, and I kept wondering what the hell was going on around me. It was the shock of it. But once I got in the court I realised this was another battle I had to win. A year on from the arrest, the trial was at Snaresbrook Crown Court, which is a very old building like a stately home. The charges were the result of a six-month undercover surveillance operation by these police officers. I believe that they didn't watch me at all, and I can't believe that they watched any of the others. The police officers just wouldn't have fit in – they would have been square pegs in round holes.

They said they had six police officers and three independent witnesses. I figured I had nine people against me, and I was on my own. What chance did I have? I couldn't see any light at the end of the tunnel. But I knew that, if I kept on believing in myself and working hard, something would come of it. And eventually it did. We were in court for 16 weeks and two days, but I didn't go in there like some of the lads who just had their newspapers and were reading. I took a notebook and pen, and plotted out a graph, pencilling in all the good points and the bad points for me and the others. Pretty soon I realised that the evidence they had was very flimsy.

They were trying to make us the scapegoats for all the trouble that had gone on before, as this was after the Heysel disaster. Chelsea's lads had got 10 years and they said we'd get the same as them. I knew I needed somebody on my side who was pretty good, and I got it in a gentleman called Paul Purnell, who was a top-quality

Queen's Counsel. I also had great solicitors in Graham Gurin and Brian Stork. Graham Gurin has become a good friend over the years and has always been there for me. We send each other Christmas cards every year, and he deals with other things for me like business details.

The brief picked by my solicitor was good – and needed to be. They said to me that the police case did not sound right. They set aside four months to hear the case against us, and it cost the taxpayer something like £5 million, which at that time was the longest criminal case in England, apart from fraud cases. But I was building this picture of what they had and what they didn't have. And it was quite evident that they had nothing. Pretty soon the policemen's logs were in question. There were apparent contradictions and inconsistencies.

There was a lot of talk from our side about the political overtones around the case. It was certainly political, without a doubt. Each prosecution witness went up and got ripped apart. We never actually got to give our side of the story, because it was slung out before we had the chance.

So our defence sent away the police logs to have them forensically tested by a method called Esda. What happens is they put chalk dust on the paper and shake it about vigorously under a machine, so that anything that's been written on the piece of paper above it shows up underneath. That way you can see if somebody's added information in at a later date. And it was found that the police had added things in after just to make it look worse. When the prosecutor found out, he decided to call an end to the case as it totally relied on the integrity of the police logs.

During the trial my dad became very ill and was in hospital. Every day I had to travel an hour and a half to court from where I lived, and get there under my own steam. I'd stand in the dock and then go home on my own. But when my dad became ill the judge very kindly allowed me to go to see him, but with two police court officers with me. It was a bit ridiculous, because if I was going to do a runner I'd have done it long before then. I was on bail and I don't do runners. So I went and saw my dad who was dying in bed, and he looked at me with tears in his eyes, because my dad was out of the old school and naturally trusted the police. To him policemen were pillars of society, but most people know that it isn't quite like that now.

My dad was the straightest man I've ever known. He was a hard-working man. One of the mornings I went to visit him on my way to court I asked a nurse, 'Can you tell me where Mr Gardner is, please?'

And she said, 'Yeah, he died at three o'clock in the early hours,' and she just walked off and left me there.

Nobody had phoned to tell me. And I had to go to court and sit there, hearing them throwing dirt at me all day long, knowing that I really wanted to be at home with my mum. I was really angry and I felt like just getting up and fucking going into one and trying to leave because I didn't want to be there. That could have been my hardest day of the trial then because you've got to hold all that in. But, if I'd exploded in court, I would have been doing exactly the sort of thing they were accusing me of. I couldn't do that, so I had to bottle it up. I was trying to suppress it the whole time. Everyone knew about it, but I was on my own, and that's the way it's been for much of my life. But I've had some great mates, some living, some dead, and I believe, if you have five good mates in your lifetime who have laid their life on the line for you, you're a rich man. I've had more than five and known some great people.

Like I say, I knew four or five of the lads who were in the dock with me, but I didn't know the rest of them from Adam. Over the weeks we were together we got to know each other because we stuck together. We were pooling our knowledge to find out what was going on. And I think as a group we did quite well. The ones I knew were intelligent people, and we picked holes in the evidence. We found several points that our briefs missed and we gave them our notes.

It was the same as when we were on the terraces – we were a team. We were in the shit together, and we dug ourselves out of it together. Or so I thought. Because it came to light that one of our lot was a grass, who tried to get himself out of trouble by grassing other people. I won't mention his name, but I will say that I hate that man. We didn't know it at the time, but we found out later. It came out that he was taken out of his cell on certain occasions and it wasn't recorded or put down in the police logs. To save his own neck he tried to grass the rest of us. Like I said before, we're family. But this bloke wasn't and never will be in my family. It was a real bombshell at the trial because no one knew until right near the end.

He was one of those I didn't know and he was a pathetic character. He tried to blame others for something that happened years before. A young Arsenal fan had got stabbed to death, and he tried to say it was Cass Pennant who'd done it. But Cass Pennant was already in prison at the time. It was impossible unless he got right through the bars and got back in there at night. That man is like shit on the bottom of my shoe – that's how I describe him. He still has the front to go to football now. I've seen him, and he's seen me. But I can't be bothered to even look at him because he's just scum. He knows who he is and may he rot in hell for what he tried to do.

Although I felt up against it, I did think I was getting a fair trial. It was just the evidence that was shit. But there were a couple of light-hearted moments in the trial. One was when one of our party was reading the paper in the back of the dock and the judge had to tell him to put the paper down. The other was when a police officer came in to give evidence and asked for a chair to sit down because he had piles. This poor police officer, who was there trying to get us convicted, had Farmer Giles and he couldn't stand up for too long. The way he walked to the box to give his evidence we thought he had asteroids not haemorrhoids! He was the one that said high-ranking police officers had told him to say this and that, and that's what opened the floodgates.

I had actually had a whole day in the dock being examined by the prosecutor. But then the next morning he said something had come to light and that the logs were not right. The prosecutor, Mr Vivian Robinson, who was a very honourable man and was very good at his job, got up and said in no uncertain terms that the police evidence was unreliable and he no longer wanted to go ahead with the trial. This was after studying a report by a handwriting expert on the police notebooks. We sat there stunned, and we were just so angry that we'd wasted all our time in there listening to all this bullshit. For four months. And then the judge thanked the jury for their patience. He said, 'Please don't think that your time's been wasted, and as a reward you will not be called for jury service for 10 years,' which I thought was quite amusing.

He then got us all up individually and told us we were not guilty of the charges against us and we left the court. The next day the papers said that when he told us we were not guilty we all jumped for joy and were cuddling each other, clapping our hands and doing high fives. But that just didn't happen. Anyone who was in that courtroom that day will testify to it. I have no time for the press, because they tried to make it look like we'd got away with it and we were jumping in the air. We just sat there stunned in silence. We couldn't believe what had gone on. There was a bit of relief, but it was mostly anger. They had taken me away from my family, and they're the most precious thing in my life. I wanted to be at home with my little boy. And they wanted to give me 10 years and take me away from them. Whatever I'd done before was not what they charged me with. Since then I'd kept my nose clean and gone totally straight.

The night before the case got thrown out I had started to think it might be dropped. The word sort of got round that one of the other barristers had said that the integrity of the police officers was in question and the Esda test had proved that notes had been added to police logs after they had been originally written. And now this police officer was making noises about the high-ranking officers. You have to be in that position to know what I was going through. You don't feel confident you're going to get away with it, but there was excitement among the barristers. Certain people let it slip that night and somebody told me they weren't supposed to say anything but I should get all spruced up because it was going to be over in the morning.

In fact, the day before it finished they left the cell door open when we had our lunch break, and we couldn't work out why they hadn't locked the door. They left it wide open. The next morning when we went down they put us in the cell and once again the door was left open, which hadn't happened in the previous 16 weeks. And that's when we thought we'd cracked it. For the first time in all those weeks we felt that there was a bit of light at the end of the tunnel, and that's how it ended up. It was unbelievable.

There were a couple of nice-looking girls on the jury who the lads had been smiling at all through the case. And then I started thinking to myself that I'd been badly treated and I must be in line for a few quid. The next day I went to my solicitor and put in a case for wrongful arrest and received thousands of pounds in compensation.

Some of the evidence was just so flimsy it was ridiculous. One part of the evidence against me was supposed to be from a hot summer's day in August. The police officer who was supposed to be with me was meant to have heard me shout, 'When you see this shiny axe in the sunlight, that's the signal for attack.' But if you're wearing tracksuit bottoms and you've got an axe down them it won't be long before your tracksuit bottoms are around your ankles. So where are the police? Do they let people walk around with axes down their trousers? I don't think so. It was made up. You could have taken four idiots to make up better stories than the ones they made up. The jury at times visibly laughed because the evidence was so poor; one woman actually told one of the police officers to shut up during the trial when he gave his evidence. She literally said 'shut up' out loud and was warned by the judge not to say any more.

They told me I was number one on the wanted list and that I was 'The General'. But when they looked at the evidence I went from number one on the indictment sheet to number three. They had to put me in the top three after what they'd said, but they found it quite amazing that I didn't have a police record.

GOOD AFTERNOON, GENTLEMEN, THE NAME'S BILL GARDNER

The trial was brought about because Margaret Thatcher had said the police had got to stamp down on football hooligans and they stamped down on the wrong people. And it was just unbelievable to hear the things that they were saying every day. There were days when we went home when we were high as a kite because we knew we'd had a good day, and another day we'd go home and feel a world of despair was on our shoulders. And no human being deserves that. The only way I can explain it to somebody is if you can imagine you've got a boy who plays at a football club: he's an academy footballer and every week they're bringing in somebody else to replace him on trial, and every week you're looking at your boy and you're looking at the other boy thinking, Is my boy better than him, will my boy be released, will they take on the other boy? And this is how I felt: one day highs, one day lows. And it was portrayed in my mood. I'd go home, have my tea, go to bed, get up the next day, bath, go to the hospital, go to the court, go to the hospital, come home. Sixteen weeks of my life. I had no money because I'd been out of work because of the two broken legs. I was self-employed and the business folded. I had no dough coming in. We struggled, but me and my girlfriend Sarah had each other, along with James, our son.

But I will go on record to say Sarah's been through more than any woman should ever endure with me. Because when you're depressed, which I was because of the breakdown I had, you are totally irrational. You are a pain in the arse and you fly off the handle at the least possible thing. How she put up with me, I don't know. But we've been together 21 years now and I think she's seen every side of me, warts and all, so we should survive the test of time.

She was always positive and knew I hadn't done anything wrong. She told her family, and I had their backing 100 per cent. My girlfriend's parents – because my dad had died and my mum was ill – became my family, and, although they knew I had a chequered past, they also knew that I've been as straight as a die since James was born. So it was nice to have that. Even though I'd only just met them, Sarah's dad is a shrewd man, and I think he knew that I was innocent, and they backed me all the way down the line.

After the trial ended I went to the first game I could. I just wanted to get back watching West Ham again. The day I was arrested West Ham had sent a banning order to my house banning me for life from the ground, which Sarah had hidden from me. She knew if I'd seen that I would have cracked up even more. When I came out she told me about it, so we immediately set about writing letters to the club.

I always thought the police might make things hard for me, which they did. For years I used to get little winks and 'hello, Mr Gardner', and I'd have surveillance cameras watching me during matches. A few weeks after the case ended I went to Luton with Sarah to watch West Ham. I saw a load of activity at the front before the game. It was about 6.45 and still an hour before the kick-off. There were loads of police officers at the front looking up at me. And this police officer said, 'Can you come round the back of the stand because I want to have a word with you.

I said, 'What's it about? I've got the right ticket, what have I done?'

He said, 'Oh, it's nothing to worry about.'

So we got up and walked round the back of the ground into the police control room and they immediately came at me from all angles. I had 16 police officers coming at me, saying, 'You're nicked. You're nicked for being the leader of the ICF.'

And I just laughed. I said, 'You've got to be joking, ain't you? I've done nothing wrong.'

And they said, 'We're acting on information we've seen.' They banged me up in a cell until 11.30 that night and then I was let out without charge.

I went to the solicitors the next day and we issued a writ for wrongful arrest. I said, 'Lovely jubbly, let's have some more money out of them.' And I got another few grand so I had a nice holiday. And this is what will happen every time they arrest me when I've done nothing wrong.

But I could only go to away games, because I was still banned. I still took my little boy James to home games and my mates would take him in and I would sit on the wall outside the ground. I knew I couldn't try to go in, as they would pick me out because of my size. I'd sit and wait outside with the surveillance camera watching me the whole time. Every time I moved up the road the camera would follow me. I came back and went the other way and the camera would still be following me.

After my girlfriend had written several letters to the club, a campaign was started by the fanzine *Over Land And Sea*. The editor Gary Firmager ran a petition that was signed by thousands of people. The supporters really got behind me.

And they let me back in 1991. They invited me up to the ground, and there I met the chief police officer in the case against me, who'd taken early retirement and got a job at West Ham as safety officer. He invited me into his office and we had a chat and he took me up to choose the seats I wanted to sit in. But it had to be in an area that they chose and they picked the most expensive ones. They sat me there, just behind the directors' box, where I had more cameras on me than there were on the pitch for the whole year.

So me and my son James sat there and it was like starting again. I went to away games for four years, but it's just not the same. And it was strange sitting there and it took quite a long while to get back into it again. I knew I would, but it took me time. And after a few years they let me sit where I wanted to, and first I moved into the family enclosure with my kids, and then on to where I sit now.

So it was all finally over and now it's water under the bridge. Anyone who knows me knows that I don't bear grudges. What's done is done.

CHAPTER FIVE

WORKING THE DOOR AT BUSBY'S

The first job I had was Busby's in 1984. It was the first time I worked on a door and I was head doorman. Somebody asked me to do it because it was a bit of a dodgy sort of place. It had had a bad reputation and so it got closed down and then was reopened. It had a reputation for having a lot of trouble, and I mean a real lot of trouble. The way I looked at working on a door was simple – I could use the extra income.

The last bit of trouble I had there was when some boys from a weightlifting club were on a beano and there were only four of us working that night. The lads had constantly been causing trouble throughout the night. They'd been warned that we'd throw them out if they carried on. They kept on, so I went down there and said, 'Right, I'm going to throw you out.'

There were about eight of them, and I thought I had the other three with me. But when I looked round I was on my own, and the biggest one said, 'What, you're going to throw us all out on your own?'

I said, 'Yeah.'

And then they said, 'Right, let's go out in the alleyway,' which was the entrance to the club. So I got in the entrance by the foyer and they've all got round me, and one of them said to his mate, 'Go on, Jim, glass him,' or something.

I ran for the door and they thought I was on my toes, but the door had two bits of loose handy angle on it. When you slammed it, the handy angle came off.

So they stood there a bit stunned, thinking I was running out the door. Instead of that, I banged the door closed, the handy angle came off and then I steamed into them. Two of them went to hospital, one with a broken wrist and one with God knows what. But, as it went off, Ted and Vaughny, who were in the club that night, came out, and unfortunately they ended up in hospital too. I was fighting with the top one, who was a boxer, and the police came and nicked us both. We both got charged and were bound over to keep the peace for a year. He was a nice feller. We met at the courthouse and we got on really well. It was one of those things. He was out of order and I was doing my job. But there was no animosity between us. The police couldn't get what they wanted because neither of us would press charges.

After that I went to work in another club in New

Addington called Russells with a doorman mate of mine called Joe Reid. He's been active on the door for years. We went up there and to be fair it was like fucking Dodge City. There were only two of us in there and anyone who knows New Addington knows it's one hell of a rough place and a few nights in there were enough for me. I went back to Busby's and told them that if they got decent blokes for me to work with I'd stay. But they didn't employ anyone decent, so I packed it in.

JOE REID
21 YEARS A DOORMAN, ON BILL GARDNER

I worked Busby's before it closed, and when it reopened we were told we had a new head doorman coming in called Bill Gardner. All we knew about him was that he came from the East End of London. There were a couple of us not too happy about that. We'd all grown up together. The feeling was, who the fuck's he? I was only 20 years old, and you know what it's like when you're 20. I thought, If he fucking starts telling me what to do, I'll fucking knock him out. But virtually from the first night he'd won us over. He just got us together and said, 'Look, boys, my name's Bill.' He told us his age, where he came from and that was it. He never said any more about his past. He just said, 'I'm the head doorman, but we'll work together. Follow my lead and we'll work all right; we'll all stick together and we'll do it properly.'

Bill's got a tremendous personality, and I think that was a mark of how good he was as a head doorman. Again, when you're in your twenties and you're still growing up, you actually really want to fight everyone. And I used to look at Bill sometimes on the door and I used to think he was bottling it. But he showed me really what door work's about. It's about getting the best result with the least amount of problems. And, if they want to think you're a fucking bottle job, then that's up to them.

I think I questioned him once when there was a bloke giving him a load of fucking grief. I said, 'Why the fuck didn't you knock him out?'

And he said, 'It makes me just as bad as any bully in the area. Anybody can clump someone who ain't up to it, or really doesn't want it. Look at him. He's pissed, he's with his mates, he don't want a row, he's just giving me loads of old bunny and I'm happy to take it.'

I did door work for 21 years eventually and he did actually fucking show me how to do it properly. It's not about having fucking massive tear-ups, it's about being diplomatic and using a little bit of psychology. You can't meet everything with a fist.

We did about three years together at Busby's and then we went up to Russells in New Addington. I went on holiday to Italy when we were at Busby's and there was a big row with these power lifters. Bill managed to get all these power lifters – there were eight or nine of them – into the foyer, and they were all jumping up and down saying, 'Let's have it, let's have it.'

And Bill shut the front doors of the club, took the beading off the door and he's gone, 'It's me birthday, boys, who fucking wants it first?'

And all the other doormen had left him. They all just backed off. And this bloke called Stocky from Epsom came at Bill. Bill whacked him with the metal and it all kicked off. It topped up it was only him and his mate Vaughny that actually fucking had it. None of the other doormen even tried to stop it. So when I came back from Italy he was on the phone saying it had all kicked off and the rest of the doormen had all bottled it.

So I came back from Italy on the Saturday and was due to work that night, and he just told me he wasn't working there any more because he'd lost confidence in the team. He had a few contacts and we got this club in New Addington: Russells. We were getting good money, but it was a fucking nightmare of a club. It was always kicking off. And he handled it right because we came out of there without a scratch and we never came unstuck even though there were loads of rows. Straight away he gained their respect. There were certain blokes there who just knew who he was and that was it.

During the time that I worked the door with Bill at Russells I remember us separating a fight between two rivals. I say us, but Bill really dealt with it. He went straight into the middle of it and just said, 'You ain't gonna fucking fight in here. Fight outside. I don't give a fuck. Once you're outside the club it's nothing to do with us.'

So they decided to take it outside, and I remember us standing there watching this fucking bloke get his head stoved in. One bloke got the better of the other and laid him out, but then he dragged him across the car park by the scruff of his neck to the back of his van, got out a metal car ramp and just started smashing his fucking head in with that.

I can remember me and Bill watching it in silence, and on the way home he said, 'We did a fucking good job getting them out because you don't need that in the club.'

We didn't stay there that long, and I know that about two weeks after we left the manager got his nose bitten off. The fleshy part came completely off. I can remember me and Bill laughing our heads off at that. I'm glad we weren't there for that one. He was an East Ender, the manager, and he was a tough old boy. I think he got involved in a scuffle because the other door team that he had weren't handling it particularly well and he got his nose bitten off.

Not so tough, even though he thought he was, was the

Welsh nightclub manager who used to give it all the time about how tough Wales was. But then as soon as it kicked off in Busby's, and he saw Bill performing, he used to fucking run. He used to shake his head, cover his eyes and run and hide in the office and come out when it was all over. And he fucking loved Bill. Without question, Bill was his hero and could do no wrong. Bill was very streetwise and knew all the tricks

In normal clubs the manager watches you like a hawk, but Bill used to watch the fucking manager. He'd have so many spies in the camp as well. You could see the manager wondering how the fuck Bill knew it all.

It was rumoured that Bill had his own fucking till on the counter. How much money did he take? And I never got a penny of it! He used to arrive late if he'd been to football, but Billy never ever used to brag about his football things. We all knew he was a West Ham supporter, but he never really gave it the big one. There were always silly little things going on in a club – just people giving a bit of lip or starting to strong it – and he'd just say one little thing to them and it was defused. He showed me that you don't have to clump someone straight off. Remember, they've probably had a drink and are with their mates. They don't actually really want to fucking fight you. What they want to do is save a little bit of face. And he didn't have a problem with that. I was the one who had a problem with that. I'd want to fucking hit everyone, but Bill was better than that in the way he did it – you don't have to meet it head on, which doesn't mean that you can't do what you want to do to that man, it just means that you're doing the professional thing and letting him walk away from you, you're not walking away from him, you're not a coward.

I tell you, no matter how bad it kicked off or no matter how bad the row was, there was always something going on for Bill. He was always happy, whether it was busy or quiet, because the fucker was making money. He loved the buzz of it, he loved working with the little team we had at Busbys, the four or five boys that were there that were solid around him, you could see him spark on a busy Friday or Saturday night when he had that core team around him, where he had the out-and-out fucking rowers and the out-and-out fucking diplomats. He could face any situation with the team that he had.

He always had time for the punters. Too many times you'd just get these arrogant fucking doormen that think they're better than the punters, and that's not the case, and Bill always showed me that. You've got to give them respect. Everybody deserves respect. And I think that's why he's so popular. Even the people that he's fucking laid out or had a row with actually respect the man because he's never taken a liberty or held that row against them or belittled them afterwards. So, even though he's fucking knocked someone out three weeks ago, it's all forgotten, and I think that's fucking brilliant.

There were a few times when we had some big rows when the Harlequin Centre was being built and it was all one big building site. We had a big row with some boys from Stockwell on a lads' night out. There were probably 15 of them and they were throwing drink about on the dance floor. We started turfing them out, and all of a sudden the main man out of their lot turned and the fight started. We were short-handed that night, but we had a pretty game old team and they were all solid boys. I saw one of the weaker doormen get hit with a really thick, heavy glass ashtray. And when you see someone holding his face, you know that pain registered with him and later on we found out he had broken his cheekbone and this bloke started to fucking go into him with his hand, so I've pulled the doorman back and I've started fighting with the bloke. It's all gone outside, but we turned them over in the end, but that was a very naughty row.

They were proper fighters, they knew the method of fighting, they weren't just street brawlers, these boys were all good fighters. The turning point of the fight was just before we got them outside, we were in the foyer fighting with them and it started to even up, it started to almost come on top for us and you just knew it was going to go the wrong way, you were starting to fucking ship a few shots. We were getting a little bit isolated, split up. But again we turned it around.

There was a boy, Sean, doorman, ex-light heavyweight boxer. Couldn't actually have a fucking street fight, but if he hit you with a shot, you'd know it. He hit this kiddie with an uppercut – when you hear the nose break, you hear that bang, bang. Fucking nose went like a concertina, claret all up the walls and again Gardner's gone, 'Yes, fucking let's go, let's go,' and then we turned it up. Fucking tremendous feeling that, to start off fighting and know it's coming on top and then, all of a sudden, bang, one little shot, we all hear it, we all see it and then there's another shout.

Bill going, 'Yes, come on.' He sensed it, he fucking knew it was gonna turn then. Just that, come on, let's fucking go. Oh, mate, everybody dug in. That was a good fight, that. We'd done them outside, we beat the fuck out of them and Bill came back with one who wanted to, I don't know, get his jacket or something.

I was walking back with the bloke that had glassed one of the doormen. I'd beaten him, we had a fucking fight, he was a tough cunt and he said, 'I like it here.'

I said, 'Oh, right.'

He said, 'I'll come back again, like.'

I said, 'Yeah, come back again, fucking bring more with you, won't you? Because you'll fucking need it.' And he was all right, he'd taken his beating.

But that was something with Bill, everybody knew that he would be with you to the death. If you had his respect, he had your respect and for me there's only a few people in life that you would say, 'No, I'll stay, I'll have it.'

'What, is it just you, Bill?'

'Yeah. No, I'll fucking stay and have it, mate, I'll stay and have it.' And there ain't too many people in your life that you go through and you think, no I wouldn't fucking leave you, never. Just situations you've been in.

That's what Bill installs around people. Confidence, he gives you the confidence. Saying that, he had a word with that boy that got glassed in that fight, got his cheek broken and had to have an operation. And it would have been very easy for Bill to just coat him off, because he bottled it basically, he swallowed it. That's what I say about respect for other people. He could have mugged him right off. As soon as he come back on the door the following few weeks later, he took him to one side and said to him, 'Look, I like you, you're a nice bloke, but door work's not for you, mate, you're not cut out for the door work, give it up.'

That's the mark of the man and he'll have respect enough for you to pull you to one side and let you walk away in a respectful way.

For a small club, Busby's used to kick right off. Honestly, it was like a fucking Wild West show when it went off. Bill was never scared of numbers and was always confident that he could control things. He'd let them know when they were coming into the club. He'd somehow find the top man in the group and he'd let them know that, if it kicked off, he would see them first. So he could control it very well, but you can't control everything all the time.

We used to do a Sunday night there and I was on the door. Two blokes came to the door and I had a bad feeling about them. You know, not the right vibes, these are Herberts. So I turned them away. They came back about 20 minutes later and they seemed to have simmered down a little bit. Bill was standing behind me and all of a sudden he's gone to me, 'He's got a blade.' It didn't really click. 'He's got a blade. He's got a blade, Joe.' And in the end this bloke's got the blade out, but luckily for me Bill had already fucking anticipated that and he's got the fire extinguisher from the foyer and just smashed it straight in the face of this mush. They were two herberts from Croydon, like two sort of rated boys.

Loads of times Bill just looked after me. People who don't know him might say that he was a bully, but I say he's never put it on offer to anybody who didn't actually fucking want it. Obviously there are times when you've got to be a bit aggressive, otherwise they take you for a bottle job. But Bill used to chat with them, have a laugh with them, and the next minute they're walking out the door themselves.

We did a private function for the local rotary club one Christmas. It was by invitation only and the Lord Mayor was there. We started letting all the local dignitaries in, and Bill's decided he's dying for a piss but he wouldn't leave the door. So he's gone in behind the counter as you pay to go in and he started pissing in the tin waste bin, which sounds like a fucking elephant pissing. It's like pouring a five-litre can of water, and all the steam was rising up and the foyer stunk of piss, but Bill was laughing his head off. As he's having a piss the Lord and Lady Mayor walked in and obviously thought that they didn't need to show their tickets because they've got their chain and all that on and it's quite obvious who they are. Bill's done no more than get a walking stick that was in this little cash room, stuck it through the slot in the glass window and he's hooked this Lord Mayor round the neck by his chain and said, 'Oi, where's your fucking ticket?' They loved it. They thought he was hysterical. And he's talking away to the Mayor and he's still pissing in the bucket with his right hand! It's one of those situations where everybody was gonna react and say, 'Oh my God, how awful, get the police', or everyone was going to make out it was the funniest thing since Laurel and Hardy. And that's what they did. They all started laughing. They couldn't leave him alone all night. They loved him. All night the Mayoress was going, 'Hello, Bill.' Only Bill could get away with outrageous things like that.

Bill's girlfriend, Sarah, moved into a flat and had a house-warming party. So we all went. I got introduced to Vaughny, 'Mad Vaughny', that was how he was introduced to me. I'd heard stories about him so I knew who he was. Got introduced to Ted and I'm there just enjoying the party, having a drink, chatting and that.

Then half-a-dozen blokes came into her flat and I wasn't really taking much notice of it. I see Bill and Vaughny go and talk with these blokes. A little bit of chat, obviously trying to get in, told they weren't gonna get in, they were pushed down the stairs, pushed out and Bill and Vaughny just followed them out. I immediately went to follow. Ted said, 'Don't worry mate, you don't have to go.' And obviously I just went.

There were 15 of these blokes outside, all fairly sort of lumpy sort of blokes and there was a bit of a stand off. All the chat had stopped and they were all sort of looking at each other. And then all of sudden Vaughny walked up to one at the front, gave him a clump and started laying into people. Bill was laughing at this stage, he was just cracking up. And he picked up this metal ladder and gave out a roar of, 'Come on,' and they ran. Vaughny was clumping everyone and Bill was just like swinging this fucking ladder about, he's hitting these blokes with the ladder, running as well, and hitting them with the ladder, knocking them over, like ten pin bowling really. I was there, but I didn't really do a lot because Bill and Vaughny were sorting it out. But that was one incident. He just treated it like a laugh, where other people would have probably thought two against fifteen weren't good odds, but he actually had that grin on his face, like he's enjoying himself.

I fancy they were probably a little bit of a firm, because they parked up a little way away, the didn't park up straight outside where people could see their motors or anything like that.

There was another time at Busby's when Bill got charged with GBH. There was this lump of a feller who had been there all night – you'd see him all the time and he was quite confident in himself. Come the end of the night and everyone was going out, but this fucker was still there. And you start to think, He's gonna be an arsehole. He's not gonna want to go. Bill was always very generous with people when he was clearing them out and a couple of us had already had a word with this bloke to drink up. But the bloke had latched on to a couple of birds.

So Bill sort of said to this bloke, 'Come on, mate, when you're ready.'

And the bloke went, 'Yeah, when I'm ready, when I've had a drink.'

Bill said, 'No, not when you're ready, mate, you've had 10 minutes now, so now it's when I'm ready and now you've got to go.'

And the bloke's gone to him, 'Fuck off, I'll squeeze your head, you fucking idiot.'

And Bill stopped. And he walked back and he said to him, 'What did you just fucking say to me?'

And this geezer said it again, 'I'll squeeze your head. Fuck off, I'll go when I'm ready.'

The bloke was probably about the same size as Bill – I'd say six foot three inches and 17 stone. He looked very smart, but you could see under the suit he was obviously a bit of a rough house. He had a few little scars over his face too. So Bill said, 'Well, best you fucking squeeze it, then.' At that moment this geezer pushed the girls away from him to give himself a bit of room. And he's just got to his feet, and Bill's hit him with a fucking peach of a right-hander. And it's actually lifted this bloke completely off his feet and over a table.

There was claret fucking everywhere, but he's got

straight back up and Gardner's gone to him, 'Now fuck off, or I will squeeze your head.' And the bloke's gone straight up to Bill again and spat this big mouthful of blood all over his face. As soon as it hit his face Bill was fuming, so he's hit him again with another right-hander. You could feel the fucking power go into it and he's knocked him fucking flying. His mouth was a mess and his lips were split. At that stage we thought enough was enough, so Bill stayed where he was and me and another doorman grabbed hold of this guy and just put him out the exit.

We all went home, and the next morning I found out he'd been in custody. The bloke went to hospital to get his face all sorted out and the nurses at casualty there called the Old Bill and then it all came out what had happened. They went straight to Bill's house, nicked him and did him for GBH. He'd knocked four of the bloke's teeth out and given him a fracture to the jaw, and all his gums and lips were split. He had to have lots and lots of stitches in his face.

So it went to Kingston Crown Court, and we were all witnesses to say that this fucker was obviously intent on throwing a shot, leaving Bill no choice but to defend himself. He got off, and I think the jury came back not guilty just because the bloke said he'd had two pints to drink, but his mate said he'd had 15 pints. Obviously they felt Bill was justified in what he did and it was reasonable force.

I can remember the first time that I actually saw Bill in

action was when we put one of the local fucking hard men out after he'd hit his bird. It's the usual shit: they've been put out the door, now they're standing there giving it what they're gonna do. They're gonna come back, do this, do that, shoot you, kill your mother – the usual stuff. And we're all standing there and taking it, and in the end Bill's got the hump with it and opened the door and said to him, 'Shut your mouth and fuck off.'

The guy's said, 'I ain't scared of you, Gardner. I'll fucking turn you over,' and all this.

So Bill's gone straight over to him and given him a big old fucking clump, and to be quite honest Bill was slaughtering the man, his legs went on the first shot, he was gone. Bill was tucking him up lovely, he was well in control of it. When you look back at it, I mean he'd slaughtered him with the first two shots, he was gone. The bloke really was just trying to hold on to Bill at that stage, he wasn't throwing anything back, he was just trying to stay up I think, trying to keep his pride a little bit. At the end of the day he had a good fucking beating by Bill really and a couple of silly little digs from me, and he decided to go.

I personally was quite happy with that. But later on in the evening Bill took me to one side and said, 'You shouldn't have done that, Joe. You shouldn't have come in to back me up because I didn't need any back-up.' Bill had a lot of pride. He didn't want anybody going back and saying, 'Yeah, well there was fucking two of them.'

And I actually took a lot out of that. If you wake up in the morning and think, Fuck me, I was such an idiot and the bloke gave me a clump, it ain't so bad. But when you wake up in the morning and say, 'Yeah, I was an idiot, but fucking five of them gave me a kicking,' you get a reprisal off that. He taught me something there.

We had a couple of tear-ups with the Grenadier Guards too. The first one was firework night when seven or eight of them were letting off bangers on the dance floor. Bill would normally go down with two or three boys that he could trust, and would give the guy the usual Bill Gardner two or three warnings. Then he'd say, 'Do it again and you're out.' As soon as we got into the foyer the DJ's calling for security. We went back down, and it was the squaddies again, so he's gone to the bloke, 'Look, mate, you've got to go now.'

And the bloke's gone, 'You couldn't put yourself out, mate, let alone me,' and he started going, 'I'm gonna cut your fucking ears off. You don't know who we are. We're fucking Grenadier Guards.'

And Bill's said, 'Look, mate, I can't hear a fucking word you're saying with this noise. Come out into the foyer and talk to me.' He's come through the double doors and he's gone to the girl on the cloakroom desk, 'Get the coats ready, because this mother's going.' He's let the double doors shut behind him and sure enough three or four seconds later this bloke's come out through the door. And he was a lump. He was probably six foot five inches tall and a right lump. Bill's hit him with a salvo of shots and knocked him out completely. The guy's gone cross-eyed and slid down the door. Bill's taken this bloke's cloakroom ticket out of his pocket, slung it to the cloakroom girl and dragged him by the scruff of the neck out through the front doors and thrown his jacket on top of him.

Then Bill's gone straight back into the club and said to the bloke's mates, 'Your mate's just had the fucking shit beaten out of him outside.'

And they've all gone, 'What the fuck's happened?'

He said, 'I don't know, mate, one minute we're here talking, the next minute some bloke's fucking smashed him.'

And of course this poor cunt's unconscious outside – he can't say nothing. And they're all round him. 'Where is he, we'll fucking kill the cunt.'

And Bill's told them, 'Someone bashed him and fucked off.'

They just bundled this bloke into a cab and went. Bill's certainly streetwise and quick with it to come up with that one.

The second time we had trouble with the Grenadier Guards, it all kicked off in the foyer. I think they'd given someone a clump outside who was nothing to do with it. In the end they were all trying to mingle in with other punters as if they weren't squaddies. Again, Bill was the general, pointing them out with his experienced eye. But they were game on for it and they wanted it, and sometimes you've got to give it.

But there was one time when Bill's teeth came out. We were having a fight with a lot of the Merstham boys. They were probably 15- or 20-handed. That was the night I got hit with a truncheon. This bloke had a lead-filled truncheon and hit me across the collarbone with it. His mates were pulling him out of the door and I was trying to pull him back in. All I could get to bite him was his arm and I sunk me teeth into his arm and he was screaming like a pig. This other doorman came out and we'd get them in a headlock and bite them on the face, neck, head, ears – wherever. We had about five or six of them laid out in the foyer, and Bill was running up and down on them laughing his fucking head off. And, as they're pouring out the doors, Bill's got one of them in a headlock and bit him. But his false teeth just fucking dropped out, just come out on the floor. Everybody stopped fighting – you ever had that split, like a comedy film where something happens and everybody stops and looks at each other?

He's gone, 'Fucking hell, I forgot I got false teeth.' We were just laughing then. And the fight's still going on but we're all laughing, fucking funny. And he finished off filling this bloke in and he picked up his teeth and put them back in.

That grin he fucking gives: 'Sorry boys.'

The nutcase that lost half his ear was another time – must tell you about that one. Big, big, big row. Again a lot of travelling boys from Epsom were involved. They're going around the club, offering people fights.

Bill's gone down, 'Look, fucking cut it out, we know you're a stag night, we know you're all together, cut it out or you're gonna go.'

'Yeah, yeah, yeah.'

And then it's got to the stage where Bill's gone, 'Right, next time you're gonna go mate, I'll put you out first.'

'Oh, you don't wanna be doing that, he'll fucking kill you, he'll kill you,' and all that. Same old shit you hear every bloody night.

In the end, we're all out on the front doors and then somebody's run through the foyer doors, reception doors and said, It's off, it's off.' So we've gone through and the place is a fucking like a Wild West show, everybody was fucking having it. One of the barmen that used to regularly join in said he jumped over the bar and clocked this one nutcase and the bloke just hit him straight back, like pinged him straight back.

'Fucking hell I realised why I was a barman and not a doorman,' he said. He was, 'Woah, I'm not getting involved in that,' and he jumped straight over the bar again. We were laughing about that afterwards. I reckon there was probably about 40 or 50 on the stag night and they were all involved all around the club in fights.

Once the main little lot had started, then they just started filling everybody in, it was right off. I've gone to go down and Bill's gone to me, 'Stay up on the high levels. Let them come to us, let them fucking come.'

This fucking nutcase who I'd seen earlier in the evening,

with mental eyes, he came up the stairs, suited, but fuck me, fucking built like an ox this cunt. I was waiting. You know, like you tee a shot off, like a golf swing, I waited for him and as he's come up the stairs, I've hit him with the chair right in the face. Nothing. Didn't fucking budge him, didn't take a backward step or nothing.

I've gone to fuck off and he's grabbed me by the jacket and he's done me with a beer mug and he hit me so hard I actually hit the deck and slid along on my back on the carpet, underneath the table. I remember one of the regular punters lifting the table and asking, 'Fuck me, you all right, Joe? What are you doing down there?'

I went, 'Yeah, yeah.'

But I got up and was straight away looking, where's Bill? And sure enough, he's still fighting with about three or four of them. They were all fighting him. And I've got up, I've done one of them with a chair again, pulling them off and then me and Bill was together again. And we just stayed there fighting our corner.

This nutty geezer that I'd hit with the chair, he had a fight with another rated bloke from this area. He done him, he'd got this bloke round from behind in a sort of a headlock, pulled him over a couch, and done him with a beer mug. But he said all the bloke done while he was in the headlock is he reached under the table, picked up another beer mug and glassed him, like bang straight in the fucking face. Then he bit him. He bit half his ear off. And he said as he was biting him, as he put his head down to bite him, the cunt was sticking his fingers in his eyes. He said he was a right hard cunt. In the end, we never got them out, as the Old Bill came in in the end with dogs and they separated us. But I mean that was a serious row, a serious row, a lot of people got hurt that night.

I don't know any of the main body of the door staff that didn't come out of that with a ripped shirt, we all had it. I had a lump like a fucking turban on me head where this geezer's hit me. Fuck me, that hurt.

Got them outside and it's still half kicking off, we're standing at the top of the steps, I've got Bill next to me. They're lobbing 50p coins at us, 10p too. And Bill's like catching them, 'Cheers mate, cheers mate'

He shouted down to this pikey, half his ear was hanging off. Bill said, 'Oi fatty,' and he looked up, he's gone, 'Are you hurt?'

He nodded his head to him, like 'Yes.'

And Bill went, 'Well, I fucking ain't, fuck off.' In the end there was a couple of arrests but the Old Bill was too scared of them to arrest them, but there was a couple of arrests.

They all went in the end and I can remember Bill saying, 'Fuck me, that was a close one.' They were a right handful, all of them could fight.

But one of them nights again where everybody stayed late that night, all the door staff and all our regulars chipped in and helped out. We all stayed back and had a drink. The manager was good like that, he'd say to you, 'Well, you've worked hard tonight boys, we'll fucking have a drink on that.' And you know when you're all sitting down telling stories, you're all fucking killing yourselves laughing, because it's funny afterwards, isn't it?

'Fucking hell, I saw him sliding across on his fucking back...'

'Fuck me, Reedy, you were hiding under the cunting table, what were you doing? Fucking geeing you up...'

But that was a serious fucking row, serious row. Again, you never see Bill, hardly ever see him one-to-one really, whereas you'd always get one-to-one somehow with someone, Bill would always have three, four, go for him. He'd have several of them think, 'Well, he's the one for me.' And he'd always have more to deal with than me or anybody else really. He was better, he was a bigger man. I suppose just the way he was he made himself a target. Maybe he was doing that deliberately, I don't know, but he made himself the target.

An experienced doorman will know you can deal with trouble before it gets in the door. The trick is to just take their attention away for a split second, then you can do what you want to do. A bloke would come up to the club wanting to fight everyone, and all Bill did was keep calm and say to him, 'Look, mate, you can't get in, your strides ain't right. Look at the state of your strides.' By the time he's looked down to see what his strides look like, Bill's clumped him and that's it.

Well, I had 21 years of doing the doors. I ended up running three clubs, and Bill was a good fucking doorman.

I've never seen him offer it to anyone that didn't actually fucking want it, and I've never seen him bully anyone. I've never seen him do anything like that. He's definitely in the top three or four doormen that I've ever worked with.

CHAPTER SIX

FAN ON THE BOARD?

That football club I support means everything to me. Always has, and always will. I saw a little disabled kid in a wheelchair with claret and blue wheels when we played Wigan away last season. We'd hired loads of Hummer limos and a big party bus and got about 60 rooms at the West Ham hotel. It was the first time they'd sold that many, and me and my mate John Waddell split all the costs and arranged everything so everyone had a good day out. And there was this little kiddie over there in a West Ham wheelchair, and he looked so happy at the end of the game. And I think that's what it means to me. He had nothing to do with us, but I saw him afterwards and I think it meant the world to him.

West Ham was my first love. When I had trouble at home, I always had West Ham. When things have been bad in my life, there's always been West Ham. It's always been the most stable thing in my life. I wish the players could see what West Ham means to that kid in the wheelchair. But they never will. It doesn't matter what team you support. Anyone in the world can sit down and say the same thing that I've just said. Let's get it right. Do you remember the last time we won anything? You've got to have a good memory.

When we won the FA Cup in 1975, the next day the team were at East Ham town hall to show off the trophy to all the supporters. It was an unforgettable day for us fans. I was right at the front – the first one there in the morning. My mum was there too, with my little girl, Kelly. We were there about six-thirty in the morning. We stayed the night in the hotel at the end of the road. The streets were packed with people, and everyone was coming up with balloons, sitting on top of lampposts and standing on roofs. It was unbelievable. Everyone was happy. Everywhere was decorated claret and blue. It was just a great time to be a West Ham fan. Those days have been few and far between, I'm afraid. But it was the best day for atmosphere I've experienced following West Ham.

We've had a few heroes at West Ham. We're not a club that wins anything, but we've got players who've played for the badge. If I was coaching a kid at football and wanted him to copy one player, it would be Stevie Potts. I was fortunate enough to be the manager of the West Ham supporters' team in his testimonial match when we played the All Stars. Rod Stewart played and my lad James played too. I've got to know Steve Potts since he retired and he's a gentleman. And he gave everything to the club. He never brought the game into disrepute, he never moaned when he was subbed, he was a true professional, and in any form of life I take my hat off to people like that. It's all right having fiery people, but at the end of the day the lifeblood of your club are people that are loyal.

If we're talking about the most skilful player I ever saw play for West Ham in the 45 years I've been watching: that is Paolo Di Canio. Paolo Di Canio for me was quality. He got the fans up and he produced moments of magic that no other player had done for a long while. I know he had his problems, but Di Canio scored some marvellous goals. Like the volley from over his shoulder against Wimbledon. It was an unbelievable shot. But the thing for me that typifies him was the game against Everton when he could have scored into an open goal but he caught the ball and stopped the game because the goalkeeper was injured. It might sound silly because we'd have won the game, but for me that summed up what we're about. We got more acclaim for him doing that than if we'd won the match and I was prepared to take that on the day. I loved the man.

When the club first bought him some had their doubts, but I thought he'd be great because I knew that Celtic fans said that he was fantastic for them, and Sheffield Wednesday fans liked him as well. It was only the incident with Paul Alcock the referee that put a dampener on him. I know what he is like, because he sent me off six times playing five-a-side. I wish I'd pushed him over too, because the bloke was an absolute arsehole.

Bobby Moore for me will always be our greatest ever player for what he achieved in the game. I mean you're talking the World Cup final captain, how can you better that? With Geoff Hurst and Martin Peters in that team too, you'd have to say that we didn't achieve the success we deserved considering the players we had. To have a quarter of that World Cup-winning team and to win zilch was unbelievable, but that's what being a West Ham fan is all about. If you're a glory hunter, you ain't a West Ham fan, that's for sure, because the only glory that we ever had was between the fans.

I used to stand as a kid on the North Bank when I first went to West Ham. In those days the crowd was made up of working-class people, and a lot of them used to work on the London docks and at Fords Dagenham. Fords Dagenham at that time had a work force of about 54,000 people. Now I think it's about 3,000. My dad worked at Fords all his working life, except when he was on the railway during the war. The people then, just like now, wanted to see their team giving everything. We can handle the losing as long as they give 100 per cent. When they cheat, when they don't give that effort, which everyone of us has given in our everyday life, we find it hard to take that they're earning the big money. All we ask is 100 per cent effort. It's not hard to do when you're a fit young man.

When I first went, people used to hang from everywhere they could to get a good vantage point of seeing the game. And you used to have to get in the ground as soon as it opened to get a good position. Back then it opened at 12.30 and it was everything to everyone. 'Bubbles' used to go up all round the ground all the time. It wasn't like now. I know 'Bubbles' is our song, but I always think it's a defeatist sort of song. I always felt that we needed something more rousing than 'Bubbles' to get the crowd going. I don't talk about fading and dying; I want to talk about winning.

Back then my favourite player was Geoff Hurst. I used to try to copy him when I played. I used to puff my cheeks out and run like Geoff Hurst. I used to like Johnny Byrne, and Harry Redknapp on the wing, with not one hair out of place on his head. I actually remember one day that he took a comb out during a game against Derby. Harry was a character. The team was full of characters.

People forget we were one of the first clubs to play black players in top-flight football. John Charles and his younger brother Clive played for us, and then Clyde Best, who was a lovely feller. Clyde Best was a teetotaller who got caught up in a drinking story at Blackpool when they reckon that West Ham players were pissed on the pitch after some of them were spotted in a nightclub the night before a game. There's been a few times since then that I thought they were pissed on the pitch, at any rate.

Three or four of our lads got caught up in this scandal of

the day. I think Bobby Moore and Jimmy Greaves were involved in it in and I forget the other two, but Clyde Best was involved.

Now everyone knew Clyde Best only used to drink orange juice. He was like the gofer, he used to run people around everywhere. I heard about times at parties when people couldn't get home and thy'd ask Clyde to give them a life and he'd go out of his way. A gentleman, a nice man. I think he's now in Bermuda where he came from. He's something to do with the Bermudan team.

But in those days you were in awe of the players. You looked at your players in those days and they were above you. If you shook hands with them, you wouldn't wash. I had lots of heroes, but I had heroes that played for other clubs as well as my own. I used to like Stanley Matthews and George Eastham, who played for Stoke City.

Alan Devonshire was another hero and I still talk to him now and again. He's manager of Hampton and Richmond in the Ryman League or the Conference. He's been there a few years and he's done really well. I don't know why he's never been offered the chance of doing something in some capacity at West Ham. He was a forklift driver from Park Royal who we bought for about £5,000, and he set the world alight over here. Next to Di Canio, he's my favourite player. His greatest game was the FA Cup final against Arsenal when he went down the wing and stuck over the cross for the goal. He just used to beat people for fun. And there was nothing to him, a very thin man, very slight character. He was crippled out of the game for months after the FA cup tie against Wigan.

Back then, a tackle was a tackle, not like now when there's no contact with the goalkeeper. In those days you could charge the goalkeeper. I remember in my youth goalkeepers used to wear big, thick jumpers, polo neck jumpers. Now it's all this high-tec fibre, breathe-easy gear and all that. Not then, I'm afraid. You wore something to keep you warm and woolly gloves. There was a bit of rubbing-in liniment you could get, I forget what you called it, but like Ralgex, the goalkeepers used to rub it on their toes and on their fingers to keep them warm in the game because their hands used to get wet all the time.

The best two goalkeepers we ever had were Phil Parkes and Ludo Miklosko. Phil Parkes we bought in the Second Division from QPR. Then it was a record fee for a goalkeeper. Phil had terrible arthritis in his knees. I've been fortunate enough to get to know both of these people and they're lovely blokes, both of them. It's hard to say which one was the best, but for me personally I'd have to give it to Ludo because I've come to know him and I've never met a more genuine man. He's a gentleman and a gentle giant. He's knowledgeable too, and probably the most qualified goalkeeping coach in the country.

Billy Bonds was different class too. All any fan wants in their team is their captain to come out and play as if he was a fan out there wearing the armband. And Billy Bonds did that. Whether he played right-back, in midfield or at centre-back, he would do the job. Billy wasn't like the normal footballer at that time, who used to go out on the piss. Billy used to get the job done and go home to his family. And I respect that, because I'm a family man and I know that's exactly how I'd be. But on the pitch – like Tony Adams when he played for Arsenal – he puffed his chest out and gave it everything. Stuart Pearce was the same. They were all a different breed. Those sort of people are few and far between.

Mind you, as I've said, he went down in my estimation when I heard he called the fans scum after the incident in Spain. That said, he was a great club captain and I won't take that away from him. My best match memory of Billy Bonds was when he got injured in a game. He had a bandage around his head and carried on with blood streaming out of his head – swashbuckling Billy. You always remember your club captains and we've had some terrific players wearing the armband. Julian Dicks did it with dignity when he was captain of the side. Bobby Moore was our greatest ever captain, but Julian Dicks was a fan in a shirt. With Julian, you always knew when somebody had upset him, because you could see him running 40 yards to get them. He wasn't very subtle in what he did. The red mist used to come down, and anyone who used to watch in those days could see it coming. He was a terrific penalty taker too.

Alvin Martin was another tremendous captain. He was a nice man too and very knowledgeable. My main memory of Alvin Martin was going into a fish and chip shop in Dagenham when West Ham played there in a pre-season friendly and he was in front of me getting his pre-match meal of steak pie and chips. And I said to him, 'Is that your meal, Alvin?'

He said, 'That's what I have every week.'

He sat in his car and he ate his pie and chips before he went to the game. And that sums up the lad. A down-to-earth Liverpool lad that never forgot his roots. He made good arrangements for his future with the office furniture business he had. And if you hear a radio commentary from him, you're hearing it from the horse's mouth. You're not hearing bullshit.

I can recall a good night out I had when I met up with quite a few of these players in the team of 1986 dinner. It was a one-off event at the Prince of Wales Hotel in Woodford. They were all there that night and we had the boxer Stevie Roberts on our table. It was a reunion for the team of 1986, which was full of characters. It was just before Glenn Roeder was appointed and the manager's job was still up for grabs. And they all wanted it. Ray Stewart had been coaching in Scotland and he fancied a go. I spoke to Alan Devonshire and he said he was a bit disappointed that he had never been offered anything up there. All these players still had the club at heart. Frank McAvennie and Tony Cottee were both there too – it was a great night.

McAvennie. What a player he was for us. He was a hero. He had his problems off the pitch, and I think he still has, but he did the business. My long-lasting memory of him is the game over at Chelsea when we beat them 4–0. I think he got one and Cottee got two. There were Hammers all over the ground. We finished third in the league that year. We weren't just beating teams that year – we were thrashing them. We were the best team in the division that year and finished third, simply because the Board didn't have the foresight to buy two or three players to strengthen the squad when we were on top. We had to play three or four games in about nine days at the end of the season and that knackered us. If we'd gone out and bought players, we might have nicked it. It was the same the following season.

Whenever I talk about good West Ham teams and great players I think of players like Pop Robson, who was for me the best finisher in the six-yard box. No one finished a ball like him. Him and Geoff Hurst would be my two front men in my all-time West Ham team. In goal, it would be out of Parksy or Ludo – I'd go for Ludo. My full-backs would be Billy Bonds, when he first came to us in 1967, and Julian Dicks at left-back. My centre-halves would be Alvin Martin and Bobby Moore. My midfield would be Trevor Brooking, Alan Devonshire, Paolo Di Canio and Martin Peters. And up front I've got Hurst and Robson. So then I'd have McAvennie on the bench. I liked Mark Ward, who was a little fiery winger and was another one who played like a fan. I think anyone who actually works at West Ham now would admit that none of the current lot would have got in the team 25 years ago.

Trevor Brooking is another player I love. Trevor Brooking was a gentleman. Always has been, always will be. He's always got time for people and is never aloof. He was a quality player too. He was never the quickest player, but he had a lovely turn with his body or a little dummy, and he had a great brain so he put through some great passes. And of course he was very loyal to West Ham, because he could have gone to Derby. Graham Paddon was another great player, who scored a brilliant goal away to Eintracht when we lost 2–1 out there in the Cup Winners Cup. I really liked him, but we had loads of them back then.

Like I say, the players don't always want to win as much as the fans do. There was a pitch invasion one year when we played an FA Cup game at Birmingham. It was a disgraceful performance by West Ham. Nearly every one of the West Ham fans up there that particular day went on that pitch. I was on the edge of the pitch on the overspill and Tony Cottee came storming over to me and said, 'What's going on, Bill? What's it all about?'

And I just said, 'We want to win more than you, that's what it's all about.'

He could never quite work that one out. Tony Cottee was a West Ham fan. He just knew me because he used to stand on the terraces as a kid. I believe he used to have claret and blue Dr Martens. I mean, to be fair, Tony Cottee said a few things about me that I wasn't happy with, but it's water under the bridge and it's forgotten. For years I'd go to all the pre-season friendlies and stay in hotels across the world, sometimes meeting players in bars.

I went to Sweden last year and watched West Ham play

a pre-season game. There weren't many fans out there. Only four of us saw every game. I was in a bar with a lad called Andy Bowers from Canning Town who has epileptic fits, and Stevie Lomas came in. And Andy had an epileptic fit in the bar. We got him comfortable but he was quite ill. So we took him on to the seats outside, and when we came back in some of the players had arrived. There was Andy Melville, Michael Carrick, Matthew Etherington, Don Hutchinson and Steve Lomas. And they sat there having their meal and Andy, who was over the fit now, wanted to go over to the table and ask for their autograph. I said, 'Let them finish their meal, Andy, and they won't mind then.'

Andy was a bit of a nuisance and had no patience and as soon as they took the last spoonful he was over there. I didn't like the attitude of some of the players – the way they looked at him. He was a lad who'd give blood for West Ham and there they were looking at him like he was a bit of shit.

On the way out I followed the players out and Steve Lomas was the last one out the door. And I said, 'Steve, can I have a word with you.'

And he said, 'Yeah, what's the matter?'

And I said, 'Tell your mates that he wasn't pissed when he spoke to you, he talks like that all the time because he has these epileptic fits. He got hit across the head with a baseball bat years ago at Chelsea, and that's the reason why he has these fits.'

And he said, 'All right, I'll tell them.'

The next night we were having a drink in this restaurant and in he came with Tim, the chef at West Ham. He bought himself and Tim an orange juice each – that's all they had to drink – and he saw us and bought us a drink and we got talking to him. And he's a lovely, genuine character. He went up a lot in my estimation that night, and I heard he went up to the other pub, where there were some lads we knew, and he bought them all a drink too. We don't want to ponce off them. I don't want anything from the players. But at the end of the day it was a nice gesture for the sake of 10 or 15 quid. There were eight people there who will always speak highly of him. I've always believed he gave his best for the club at all times, but I think now that maybe he is a man approaching the twilight years of his career. With the money they're earning now, I don't know if players need testimonials. When you finish your working life, nobody says, 'Come here, Bill, I want to give you a testimonial.' You know you've earned your money throughout the years and that should be it. Let's get it right: they earn good money. Players in the lower leagues earn a lot less. I had a mate of mine who was a second-year professional at Wycombe Wanderers, and he was only on close to 400 sovs a week. And that's not good money. He's now captain of Crawley Town and he's an Irish Under-21 international. He was one of the lads I found when I was scouting. He's a quality feller. He was offered a new contract by Tony Adams but didn't take it.

Testimonials are something that have almost gone out of the game now, as they were usually for players that had been with a club for 10 years, and that's unheard of today. Bobby Moore's testimonial against Celtic was the best one I remember. It was a fantastic atmosphere and a great game. Geoff Hurst's one against a European XI was also good. And then you had the Billy Bonds one against an Irish XI.

As a club we have not had many managers. The best manager we've ever had was Johnny Lyall. He was everything that we wanted. He came through the ranks from office boy to coach to manager. He had the respect of the players, and he had the respect of the fans, but he was shat on by the club. I don't think he's been back to the ground since the day that they got rid of him. People thought he was losing his way in the last few seasons – a bit like Harry Redknapp. I think that a manager's shelf-life isn't that long. I think two or three years at one club's enough, because the players hear the same team talk, the same wind-ups, the same things, year in and year out. But the exceptional ones, like Sir Alex Ferguson and Brian Clough, can keep it going. Clough was always my hero. I've been a manager myself for over 33 years – kids football and adult football – and Clough was the manager I always wanted to be. I wanted to be Bill Gardner with a little bit of Brian Clough added in. I like to bring a bit of humour to the training ground. I think I've done that over the years.

Some of the players I've managed could tell some stories. The first year I ever managed a football team, the team went out and lost 8–1 in the first game. And I wasn't happy. I'm not going to name them, because it's a bit embarrassing for the lads. I attacked them with a chair in the showers afterwards because I didn't think they gave enough effort. I lost the ones that didn't have the bollocks, and the ones that stayed played for over 150 games. At the end of the day I want to win. I'm not in anything to lose.

I managed three local football teams – Woodhatch FC, Horley Town and Battlebridge Boys. It was a real pleasure to work with these lads. Woodhatch FC won everything in Sunday football except the National Sunday Cup. We were first-class. The team was made up of lads who all supported different sides and we have remained good friends ever since. With Horley Town, we were always in the top three in every division that we played in, and in my last game we won the cup 1–0 against all odds against the league winners, who were a bunch of bullies. Three of my lads had to go to hospital after the match with injuries. Battlebridge Boys gave me the most pleasure of all. When I took over with my son James, I was told that we would never win a match. Well, we proved them all wrong, winning two championships in a row!

I also managed the Crawley League district side with my assistant, Barry Marcham. We took the lads to the league's first cup final in over 50 years, eventually, and somewhat unluckily, going down 2–1 to the Tandridge League. Coaching at a primary school for 10 years with kids aged four to seven was also a high point for me. To see kids enjoying their football gave me a real buzz. In one presentation assembly at the school I had 150 children singing my name in a song that they had made up for me. Great kids! I miss them all.

I also won a Community Award, which was sponsored by British Gas, for my service to youth football. And I was a scout for Wycombe Wanderers and Crystal Palace for seven years. It was only ill-health that put a stop to all this, but that's life. My good friend Cass Pennant arranged a party for me in the West End of London. Hundreds of people turned up, and not only West Ham fans. They all believed that I was going to die. I had been ill for a long time, but I looked on my illness as another fight I had to win. And now, after losing five stone and with regular visits to the gym, I'm pulling through and winning the battle... but only time will tell if I have done enough.

Ron Greenwood was a shrewd tactician and a good manager. He went on to manage England. But then we started the steady decline down. Harry Redknapp did all right for us, but Harry was Billy Bullshit for me. Billy Bonds was a great coach but I don't think he could have done it at management level because people never lived up to his expectations as professionals. They weren't as professional as him. And he couldn't handle that. It's very hard for people that are used to being at the top of the tree in their game to put up with people that aren't putting it in. And I think that's what it was with Billy Bonds. He knew he was on a loser with these people. And then you've got Glenn Roeder who was supposedly picked for the job. I think he probably was the only one who wanted the bloody job. Glenn took a lot of stick. But I don't hear one person that I know at West Ham say a bad word about Glenn Roeder. They all say he's a nice bloke and that he did the best he could. If your best isn't good enough, we can handle that. But I think he wasn't treated that well. He had trouble with the Board.

And then there's the current manager, Alan Pardew. What can I say about Pards? I did an interview with Alan Pardew for the fanzine *Over Land And Sea*. He's a very good PR man is Alan Pardew. He talks to you like he's been a West Ham fan all his life and he's your long-lost mate. He's got a mate who's a West Ham fan, who I think tells him things about how the fans feel. But I think his mate only goes to home games. He doesn't know how the fan who goes home and away feels. When I did that interview, after 10 minutes I could see through the man. And, if the players see through him the same way I did, then no wonder we've got the problems we've got.

I'd rather the team took two steps backwards to come three forwards than the way it is at the moment. I believe a lot of the players are overpaid and they've all become big-time charlies. You only have to pick up the paper to see that every team's got them. You've got all the things that go on all the time like these roastings. I mean, in my day the only roast you had was roast potatoes and roast meat for your dinner on a Sunday if you were lucky. But now you've got all these birds getting roasted. You hear these stories about Cristal champagne at £150 a bottle, and I know that in the past you used to see some of the players out drinking. The difference today to me is the modern-day football player lacks character.

David Cross was a very intelligent man who came to West Ham. He was very low on ability when he came, but he improved over the years and did a fine job. Especially when he scored four goals against Tottenham one night. They might not have been the best goals you'd ever see, but I don't care. That was a great performance. But, once again, he was a character. You'd see Keith Robson playing a game of snooker with the locals. They were real people. The man didn't play as many games as he should have for us. He was a battling, tricky winger with a lot of aggression and a fair amount of skill. He liked a beer, but I thought he was a good player. Probably the best time to have been a West Ham fan was the early 1980s when we had lots of good players and good characters. But now all you hear is people moaning and groaning. Nobody's happy, and I wonder where the next generation of West Ham fans are coming from, because when you go away from home now you don't see many 17- to 21-year-olds. They've decided that they've got better things to spend their money on. What do you do? Do you spend £60–£100 going to watch West Ham on a Saturday, or do you have a couple of nights up the disco where you can have a few beers and pull an old Reenie. At the end of the day you want a return. And a lot of people feel very let down by the Board they have now at West Ham.

Years ago when we were in the top flight the Board at

West Ham were happy if we were halfway up the league and maybe reached the quarter-final in the cup. They would judge that a success. For a West Ham fan that was never success. We wanted to go to Europe. We wanted to go into the big games and beat teams. I went to Liverpool every game from 1965 onwards. We've only won there once, in 1964, and I didn't go. From 1965 onwards we've never won at Liverpool. We got a few creditable draws but never won, and that sums up the attitude of the Board. Happy to be mediocre and mid-table. Take advantage of the good hearts of the fans, who they knew would always turn up. And now I think that the penny's beginning to drop that some of these good-hearted fans are saying, 'Hold on a minute, we've had enough. I'm not going to be taken the piss out of any more. I spend my hard-earned money on a season ticket, but you're not gonna get it next year.' I know loads of people that won't be renewing their season tickets next year. I myself have four and I'm only having three next year.

I've been a shareholder for nearly 10 years and I've been to the meetings. The West Ham Board have to have an Annual General Meeting under company law but, if they could do it behind closed doors without us lot being there, they would. I think they treat us with contempt. I've sat there, I've watched it closely, I've monitored the chairman's attitude and I've monitored the looks the Board give. To be honest and truthful with you, I don't dislike Terry Brown, the current chairman. He likes a laugh and a joke and sometimes I think I tickle his humour, and he's always been polite to me. And I know he loves West Ham with a vengeance. He's over there watching the youth-team games on a Saturday morning at Little Heath, the same as I am. So I don't necessarily have the same outlook as a lot of West Ham fans you hear that want Brown out. I've seen a different side to him than most of them. But, if he loves West Ham as much as he says, maybe he should say, 'I've been at this club long enough now and maybe it's time I handed it on to somebody else.' But I don't believe he'll leave with the money he's earning. Who would? For us it's a love, for him it's a business and a love.

The Board have got to take a gamble; they've got to say, 'Look, things aren't right, maybe we've got to start again. We spend a million and a half a year on our academy and the academy's the lifeblood of this football club. And it's got to be made even better than it is now.' They've got some fabulous people working at the academy. They're lovely people and genuine West Ham fans. Some of them have 40 years' service at one football club.

The club's gone into decline as it is, and I think the reason is that they've not speculated to accumulate. There was a lot of money spent on a lot of players in Harry Redknapp's reign. Then there's the hotel. I've stayed over there two or three times but that's only because I'm a West Ham fan. If you had the choice of going there or a Travel Lodge, you'd go to the Travel Lodge. What football's all

Congratulations, gentlemen.

My ICF green flight jacket. Classic.

Top: All of us, together as always.

Bottom left: James, Danny and me. All good boys.

Bottom right: Top-of-the-world feeling on the way to the Metz final.

Top: West Ham United FC junior U10s, including my son James.

Middle: Horley Town Minors. The U11s in 1994, James is in the front row.

Bottom: Battlebridge Boys U12s in 2002. My son Dan was the goalie.

Top: Dovers Green School football team (includes kids with special needs).

Middle: I managed the Crawley League Representative Team in 1998. At the centre is Ian Simpenba.

Bottom: Woodhatch Football Club with Dave Gray (top row, far right), the bravest man I ever knew.

Top left: Joe Reid – 21 years a doorman.

Top right: I was head doorman at Busbys.

Bottom: Solid friends – Carlos and Ted.

Top left: Solid heroes.

Top right: My first love, my everything.

Bottom left: The Boleyn – still a landmark

Bottom right: At Snaresbrook Court, I went on trial for my life.

Top: The generation game.

Bottom: From left to right, friend Steve Bean, John Lyall and me with the 2nd Division FA Youth Cup trophy.

about is using what you've got wisely and there's lots of things they could have done with that ground. They could make a nightclub out of the ground, they could have car boots in the car park and they could have theme nights. You could bring the community in with an Asian night, with Asian music sponsored by Cobra beer or Kingfisher beer and the local Indian takeaways. By God, there's enough of them round here. So why couldn't we do that? Then there's the weight facilities at Chadwell Heath which could be hired out to the public when the club are not using them. So, instead of going to the gym and paying their £400–£500 membership, people could pay £200 to West Ham and use the gym facilities when the club are not using them. It's the same with the astroturf pitch and all the rooms over at West Ham, which could be hired out when they're not being used.

Last season people suggested having a fan on the Board. A fan on the Board is a great idea at every football club, but you don't want a fan who's going to go on the Board and be bought. A lot of the fans will go on the Board with all the best intentions, but they get a few bucks waved in their face and they might forget the motive of why they wanted to be there in the first place. I would have loved to be a fan on the Board at West Ham. Terry Brown respects me because he knows I go to all the games and he knows that I'm West Ham through and through. But he wouldn't want Bill Gardner on his Board, because I'd say it as it is. We need a voice. We need somebody to go between the Board and the fans. When the fans have got a gripe they hit a brick wall. Nobody does anything. They moan and nothing seems to come of it, although I do know that when people write to Terry Brown he answers nearly every letter that's sent to him. In the meetings he's never ducked a single question. Sometimes I've come out of the meetings and thought he's absolutely slaughtered them today. And he's done that quite a lot. The man doesn't duck a question. I think that he fights his corner. That's what I like about him. But I wouldn't say I love Terry Brown or I'd want him in the trenches with me.

I think he's done as much as he can for the club and I think it's now on a spiral going downwards and if we don't watch out we could become the Sheffield Wednesday of the South. I think that the fans have had enough. The club has always relied on the fans, who we know are all going to be there no matter what shit is thrown at them. But that attitude's now dying, and it's dying quicker than I ever thought it would. Of 100 people that used to travel from Elm Park to the game when I was a kid, I'm the only one left.

And when the fans have really and truly had enough, they will have a say and influence. It's happened here before. You only have to look back to the bond scheme the club tried to introduce during the 1991/92 season. I was a founder member of HISA, which is the Hammers Independent Supporters Association. We just wanted the club to be fair with us. They said you pay us a certain amount of money and this guarantees your seat on your existing season ticket for X-amount of years. Arsenal tried it and I think it went quite well. But the way it was put to us was: have it, or you lose your ticket. They were pushing the fans into a corner, thinking we would suffer everything. But the fans said, 'No, we ain't having it.' If they'd come out and done it in a diplomatic way and got everyone together and said, 'Look, we're skint and we need help. We think we can do it this way. What do you think?' I think the fans would have backed the scheme. But they didn't, and there was a fans' protest organised. I was banned at the time but I watched it from afar, and I had people telling me what was going on. And the fans turned it around. It's the same now. At the end of the day, we just need freshening up.

Supporting the Hammers, like I have done, I guess you become accustomed just to having hopes. Today my hopes are for West Ham once again to have the best youth academy in the country, where we're getting kids that are coming to us because they want to play for our club, not for a pound note. I'd like to see players going out there and playing for the team and the fans. And meaning it when they kiss the shirt. It's the same at every football club – the players are there for the money and the money only. And don't be fooled by anything else. If somebody offers them £200 a week more, they're gone. I'd like to see us in the top half of the Premier League. To hope for any more than that would be asking too much. I'd like to see us every now and again have a cup win. I'd like to see us every now and again maybe just getting into Europe or the Intertoto Cup, and I don't think that's too much to ask. That's not being too optimistic. I would like to see the Board having ambition and I would like to see the players with fire in their belly. I would like to see an animated manager at West Ham, rather than somebody who just sits there with his arms crossed and doesn't say anything. I want to see a manager who's a manager, and not one who's dictated to by a high-paid player who takes the piss out of him and calls him names behind his back. I want to see a man who's a man, so, if a player's giving him stick, he'll take him in the showers and give him a good hiding and show him who's boss. I want somebody who can stand up for himself, like Sam Allardyce or Graeme Souness.

The manager I'd like to see at West Ham is somebody that nobody's heard a lot of and he's a Dutchman called Co Adriaanse. He's taken AZ Alkmaar to the top of the Dutch League, and I got to know him many years ago when I was coaching. I did a coaching course over at Wycombe Wanderers, and he put on a session for all the coaches. Coaches from all over southern England were there. The session he put on was brilliant, but unfortunately not many of the clubs grasped it. At these seminars a lot of the coaches just turn up to say hello. I got talking to him after the session and I grasped what he was on about. I was only a scout at the time for Wycombe Wanderers and a Sunday League coach, but I grasped it when a Premier League scout and coaches didn't seem to understand what he was going on about. He was on another planet. But the man's done brilliantly. He was youth-team coach at Ajax where he had to supply one player every year to the Ajax first team, and he did that for many years. He then went to Willem II Tilburg, but unfortunately it didn't go right for him there. He's now at AZ Alkmaar and he's one of the most respected coaches in Holland. And I believe he would be the man to turn it round for West Ham. He's fluent in English and a great coach, and he would have no problem settling in. He's a man with real passion and real knowledge of the game. A real football man.

I still think about what happened at Cardiff in the play-off final of 2004. The fans were superb and it was a great day out. I went down the day before with my missus and my two sons. We stayed in Newport at a little bed and breakfast with a group of friends. There were about 10 or 12 of us in all. We went out that night and had a few beers. We had all the feeling of a great day and then the bitter disappointment of losing. The worst thing about the day was the game. We went there with big expectations. We were up against Crystal Palace, who will never be as big a club as West Ham as long as they've got a hole in their arse. I knew of fans that were being offered tickets for free. I think one school in Biggin Hill were given 400 tickets because Palace couldn't get rid of them. I knew people that worked with my missus who had never been to a game that season and they were all getting dressed up in Palace gear.

The West Ham turn-out was unbelievable once again. People went there with hope in their hearts. Three, sometimes even four, generations of West Ham fans were there. You saw people you hadn't seen for years. There was a great atmosphere before the game and we took over Cardiff town centre. I had a front-row balcony seat, and when the players came out, well, I can only say that I could have picked 11 fans off the terraces that would have given more in terms of effort that day. Only one or two players came out with credit. Steve Lomas and maybe one other. But the rest of them flopped and they know it. They picked the biggest game of the season to put on their biggest flop. And it made me think, Did they really want to go up?

Tactics? Well, let me sum this up. If you go 1–0 down and you take three strikers off with 20 minutes to go in a game that could go to penalties, do you really want to win the game? It was the first time that we'd made a profit for years. We got to the final and the team maybe gave 30 or 40 per cent effort. Nobody can say they gave any more. The fans were heart-broken. It still hurts now just thinking about it. Oh for another night like at Metz for the final of the Intertoto Cup. It was a fantastic night and there must have been 4,000 West Ham fans over there. It was the first time I'd taken my boy James to an away game. He loved it. It was a great atmosphere afterwards in the bars in the city centre. We took over the place. And not one bit of trouble. It must have grieved the police. There was all these East Enders making the trip, and there was not one bit of trouble.

I don't know whether my ideas will ever be taken on board at West Ham. But maybe if people read this book they might just strike a chord.

CHAPTER SEVEN

WHAT THEY SAID

*Sometimes the name Bill Gardner and his reputation
are bigger than the man himself. You've only got
to look at the amount of hoolie books that attempt to
justify their own worth by using Bill's name.
There's been plenty said about Bill Gardner, but
until now he has never really spoken...*

I wasn't ever going to have this book written, but people
have used my name in other publications and I feel it's
only fair that I get to fight my own corner. It's one of the
reasons that this book has come out. Be under no illusions:
I haven't had this book written to give money to Third
World countries and their needy, needy people. I've done
this book for me so that I can answer some of the critics.

I'll start with the book *Hoolifan*. The author states that at
Chelsea I took a punch that knocked me down the stairs.
This didn't happen. The Chelsea fans did try to give me a
slap, but two people, Carlton Leach and Johnny Butler,
jumped in front of me and took the punches for me, for
which I'm eternally grateful. In another part of the book it
states that me, Cass Pennant and Andy Swallow were spotted
at a service station and that we were chased down the

motorway by an 80-strong mob of Chelsea fans. I can categorically state that I've never been in any vehicle with Andy Swallow. I have with Cass Pennant, but never with Andy Swallow, so this is all just to give the book a bit of credence by bashing my name out again. Anyone who knows me knows that I can't walk properly, let alone run, so that's absolute nonsense. Neither myself nor Cass was ever involved in that incident, and Andy remembers a different version of events to what they say happened that day.

In the book *Among The Thugs*, it was stated that a Manchester United supporter, Roy Downs, threw a hot cup of tea at me, which he did. But I moved out of the way and only got caught by a little bit of it. We were at Stoke and Manchester United were playing at home, and all this carry-on happened at Euston Station. Roy Downs was a loudmouth and a bully. He tried it on with a young West Ham fan and I pulled him on it, and that's when he threw the cup of tea at me. But, as I say, it missed. I heard later that day that he was seriously hurt on the way back. I can only presume that he'd got up to his old tricks again and upset somebody else, and they'd done him. Good job – the man was a bully.

In *Steaming In*, it states that I made a phone call to Chelsea saying, 'I'm sorry I can't be with you this week but I'll see you next week,' which is absolute rubbish. I did not make this call. Somebody may have made this call using my name, but it was not me.

The *Soul Crew* book said I told Cardiff fans to get their

toy-town firm off the platform at Birmingham. That might have happened and, if they were all pissed up and being silly, that's what I would have said to them anyway.

Somebody told me to read the book *Red Army General* because there was a chapter in there on West Ham and my name was mentioned more times in this book than God's mentioned in the Bible. Tony O'Neill wrote this book but I call him Tony Who? Because who was he? He said he was leader of the Mancs. And all I can say is he was so well known that he was bashed by one of his own fans. What a mug. He sounds like a pissed-up northern bully – always being nicked or bitten by poodles. Good job he never faced me or I'd have sent him running home to his mum for back-up. Let's go to the things he's written. Man United had crowds of 68,000 and West Ham had crowds of 25,000–30,000. In his book he states that West Ham always left the ground early to avoid being bashed on two sides by Man United's Red Army. Well, of course we're going to leave early. Who's going to lead their people into a trap? Certainly not me.

When we did go to Man United, as people that have been there will know, you came out just that few minutes early all together, and you made your way back down to the station so that they can only come at you from one side. I wouldn't have them coming at us from two sides or three sides. What sort of idiot is this bloke? No wonder he never got the job done. We were always outnumbered when we went up to Man United – 10 to one in some cases. They gave you the bare minimum tickets they could. That would be just 1,200–1,800 tickets. He talks like there were an equal amount of us and them. That just didn't happen. If you went up there, no one got hurt or nicked, and you took the piss out of them all day long, that was a result. It was job done. Man United never got the job done with us. That's no lie. That's the way it was. And I don't know why they can't speak the truth.

Our plan was always to go up there, frustrate them and out-think them, and we always did it, year in and year out. But they were such a predictable, noisy, mouthy, unorganised rabble. The boys that liked to drink used to find a pub and we would camp out. No one would come to confront us. His reason for them not having a go at us because we had weapons doesn't hold any water. No one carried weapons. Would the police not stop and search for weapons if they thought people were carrying them? He's trying to make it out that everyone carried weapons when they didn't. Nobody carried weapons, and it's just not feasible that they wouldn't search a large group of blokes.

Tony Who? says he saw me many times at the front of the firm. Why did he never front me on his own? Because the man was two-bob. Front me? It seems to me he's only good at CS-gassing himself. He talks about us carrying weapons, but in his own words he says he had a CS-gas canister that he actually gassed himself with. So, if he isn't gassing himself, he's getting bitten by a poodle. He was ravaged by a police dog. Unbelievable! He mentions a situation in 1982 when he says I met a bloke called Harry the Dog at the World Cup in Spain. Not true. The only person I met in Spain was Micky Greenaway, a lifelong Chelsea fan and man with honour. He's now deceased, God rest him. Do you think that I would say in the heat of the battle, 'Shh, we've had enough, get them off us'? What a load of shit. I'd rather die than say that. Not true. And he should know it.

In his book he also says, 'Gardner and his boys were off swinging punches and although the United boys had a go, they were obliged to back away.' I think he's used the wrong word. Instead of 'obliged to back away', he might have said 'obliged to run for their lives'. TV footage will confirm what I am saying. On page 206, he blames bad support at our place in 1983 on train disruptions and bad weather. What kind of excuse is that? Let's go to the ferry incident. I was already in Holland when this ferry went, but I had several friends that were on it. Twenty of my friends were on this boat, including a man well into his fifties at that time. There were 150 Man United fans on this boat and he's trying to say that they were all goody two-shoes. Well, why is it that they all got pissed getting out of the harbour and then repeatedly attacked the 20 West Ham fans that were on the upper deck until they were beaten back so many times that one of them actually appeared with a white handkerchief in his hand to surrender? Why do you think they were going over – to look at the bulb gardens in Holland? He tries to make every excuse under the sun rather than tell it how it was.

I went to the first game we played at Old Trafford after the ferry incident. We had a good day out and nothing happened, and Manchester United supporters didn't seem to have the interest. Once again, Manchester United never got the job done. I hear that he now runs a travel business. If that's so, I'd be careful about booking with him to go to America, because you might end up in Italy. What a mug! If he'd have been a West Ham fan we might have given him a job as a teaboy.

CHAPTER EIGHT

NOW IT'S OUR SAY

*T*he year 1980 was a good one as a West Ham fan, as was 1975. We won things and we also won hearts and minds, both on and off the terraces. It would be difficult to imagine what those times were like unless you were there, for we are talking 30 and 25 years ago. There will be a generation today reading through the pages of this book and wondering if it all really happened. And this one man, William Gardner, can such a character be believed? It would be fair comment if you were to see Bill today: this very private family man, who just loves his football and his sport, whether at grass-roots level or at the professional echelons.

Forget Bill for the moment and look at today's football scene under the glare of CCTV surveillance cameras, heavy stewarding, banning orders, Section

60 and NCIS with their police spotters. They have all contributed to reducing the trouble to such an extent that today you would only hear of the odd event via mobile phone or on a website. It would be understandable if you took the view that the events described in this book are entirely unimaginable. Is it possible for one man to stand out with such an aura and to gain the respect of both friend and foe? Unless you were there, and unless you knew the man, you perhaps wouldn't know or believe it. But we know, don't we? For there are still plenty of people from the generation that can remember going to football during the heyday of the 1970s and 1980s. They have their own memories conjured by the mention of the name Bill Gardner. The accounts of derring-do will just flow without the need of any prompting.

TED

Bill was definitely a loner. He's never had his own firm; he just attaches himself to people. He attached himself to the Mile End, and with them we made up the Teddy Bunter firm at roughly the same time all those years ago.

One story I remember, not particularly about Bill, but just about all of us, was the time we'd got in the Shed and we kept quiet. We got our little bit of the ground and that. And you're never sure who's with you. You're just hoping there's enough of you and then someone would start Bubbles up, that's the old classic isn't it, and then they'd just know we was there and then a gap would open and we're like one side and they're the other.

This particular time I remember once it started, we just went from our side of the Shed and pushed them as far as we could and then it's just this dirty great gap. And there was just one Chelsea bloke who stayed there, Kojak, people might remember him. Black geezer, bald head, Kojak. He was the only one who stayed there and because he stayed we left him alone, we didn't touch him. Because there's one thing about us– it's just one of those things.

And I was there for the famous one. Now this is the one where there might be some confusion – I'm sure it was a Saturday afternoon and we'd had fights with them all day long. We got into the forecourt and we thought we're outnumbered. And then Bill just come out and said 'Good afternoon gentlemen, my name's Gardner, who wants it?' And as soon as he said that, the Old Bill nicked him.

It wasn't healthy for us because the Old Bill just nicked him straight away and we're still stuck in there with them. You had to be there to witness it when Bill mentioned his name. They just stood back and we were just astonished by their reaction – the joke of it was the Old Bill was right next to him, so it was a stupid nicking. And apparently that was the first time he'd ever been arrested at football.

Now the only place we couldn't get in that day was the Shed, so me and all my lot have all gone and got in the sides and once we got about one or two hundred of us in there, we went from one end to the other. We just completely took that side. I don't know how we got them, but West Ham bought tickets for the other side and completely took it, I mean, really done the business over there where their top boys were supposed to be, but we had plenty of fun over on our side. That was the day where we had three sides of that ground, as far as I'm concerned. But the only place that we didn't really have a connection was the Shed because we just couldn't get in there.

I also remember down at Southampton we sometimes used to be able to get into their end. This time for some reason there weren't many of us in their end. I'd say there were no more than 20 of us, and they sussed out we're West Ham because our faces don't fit. They're just like Tarzans. I mean, we're big, aren't we, and they were all like our size round us. They were having little pops at us, and we were just so outnumbered you couldn't do nothing. And they were really humiliating us, really making us feel bad. And at the time I was wondering what's going to happen here. We managed to survive to half-time, and it was still not looking good, but for some reason they hadn't done us.

And we were really keeping quiet, you know, just taking it all about West Ham scum and all sorts – really bad news. I don't like being humiliated. To me there's nothing worse. I'd sooner you hit me than humiliated me. And we couldn't do nothing back because we'd have got slaughtered.

And this had gone on through the whole match. I think

we lost 1–0 which was quite fortunate because we didn't have to cheer our team. Come the end of the game we were fuming because we'd been humiliated for 90 minutes. We just took it all. We were just like sponges. And then come the end of the game they still hadn't done us. So they've all gone bowling out and by this time I think a few others have come from the sides. They knew we were there and I suppose there was about 30 of us. They were all in front of us and we've gone maniacal. I've never fought so well in my life. Because it just built it up inside of me, the anger of being humiliated and that, and once we got behind them, even though they outnumbered us like five to one, we just went straight into them and did them. And we ended up chasing them all around the place. Just our little lot – 30 or so. Bill was there, Cliff was there, I think Haystacks was there. And their lot were all like bodybuilders, you know, they were Tarzans.

And once we got out of that ground we turned into fireballs. We turned into supermen. We were behind them, which is always better if you're gonna attack someone. And so we went into them and they just ran away. And then all over the town it was going off. It was just one of them. Sometimes when you had no right it would work out for you still.

I can go back a long way with Bill. But I will say this: Bill was a different persuasion to me. He's a West Ham fanatic, isn't he? He's not just about fighting. To me, he's Mr West Ham. When you talk about West Ham, it's him.

GOOD AFTERNOON, GENTLEMEN, THE NAME'S BILL GARDNER

STRATFORD NOEL

I remember a time at Boro. I think it was 0–0. We were in the corner and we came out and I remember the street was empty. It was all terraced houses and we were walking along the street and this little firm of Boro appeared from around the corner. Everyone was on to chase them. I remember Bill saying, 'Don't run, don't chase them, it's a trap.' And we just carried on. And as we turned the corner they were all over in the little park with the old-fashioned wall, and they just started throwing bricks and we were pinned up against the wall. And then Bill shouted out, 'Right, now, let's do them,' and everyone to a man vaulted the wall and chased them all through the park, all through the city centre.

They were still trying to throw bricks. We just went through them, chased them all across Ayresome Park, chased them all through there back into the city centre. We only had a small firm but we ruled the roost that day. And as I say we were only youngsters and we thought we'd won a war.

After chasing them through the park, we couldn't find them. They were coming up the side streets. But they wouldn't come out into the main drag. We couldn't run anywhere. There must have been at least 300. If it hadn't been for someone like him taking charge, saying stick together, no one run, I think we would have all took a pasting. One way or another we would have all got done. It was the first time I really noticed Bill. I wondered who it was, and it wasn't until two or three days later that I actually found out who it was. It was Gardner.

In 1974, when Man United were relegated, their first game in the old Second Division was away, and we had Man City away. I remember me and Hampton met up heading towards Euston and someone came out and said we can't get in because there was hundreds of Man United Cockney Reds. They were on their way to Orient and me and Hampton had to walk all round and then we met Bill. And Hampton said to Bill, 'We can't get in the station; we can't go to Man City,' but we knew Morgan and that were already in there. There was Stevie and I think Matty was there. I can't remember the other names.

But Bill said, 'Fuck 'em, I'm going to watch West Ham,' and we proceeded to follow him. He marched in the station right through the concourse and Stevie Morgan and that were all over by where the bar is now, and United surrounded us. And we didn't know what we were gonna do because the Old Bill didn't want to know – there wasn't such a thing as an escort then. And Bill pushed his way through. We went right through the concourse to get to our platform to get the train. That was another time when Bill's presence was all it needed, because otherwise I know for a fact I wouldn't have gone to Man City.

Bill used to do his own thing, because I don't remember him much from doing anything special when it would go off over West Ham. I don't think anyone had the balls to come over to West Ham and have a proper pop. What little firms had turned up over the years are not really worth bothering about. I'm sure Bill probably thought to himself, Well, someone else can deal with that. It was the away games I remember him at.

I remember going to Liverpool one year and it was my first time there. I was on the train and I was shitting myself. I went to the toilet and Bill was in our carriage and he went, 'What's the matter?'

I said 'I'm not shitting myself,' but the nerves were at me. This was on the way, just pulling in.

And he went, 'Don't worry, you'll be all right.'

It was the first time we took a big mob up. A massive one. I think we took three trains. It must have been winter time because it got dark quickly. We came out after the game and we were walking down the road and there were cries of 'Stay together; don't chase them.'

And I can remember a little firm came out in the corner. Same sort of thing as Boro. And people were saying not to chase them. But, of course, with a big firm like that, people do. And I ended up chasing someone and I got down the bottom of the road and it all went to pieces. I couldn't understand it because we'd done well at Anfield Road. We had a good firm there and we outed them. That gave everyone a good gee. Liverpool had a lot of their boys in that end. And we ran them when we first came outside. Our mob were not altogether; everyone was doing their own thing. I think if it had been a nice tidy little crew of say 50–100 it would have been OK. But the firm was too big. It was the biggest away firm I've ever seen and it was too disorganised. It might have been Bill saying not to chase, but we did. Our whole deal of going away was to get back – to survive.

And where the respect came from was that everyone had a pop at West Ham because we didn't have numbers like Tottenham and Chelsea away, so they all came at you, didn't they? Then they found out that we would stick and that's what gave us this rep. In the 1980s we were rolling everything so people just didn't want to lose. So that's where the weapons came out because West Ham didn't want to lose that reputation. But it was them that got that reputation in the first place in the 1970s. It was the small little units – the Morgans, the Hamptons, the Bills, the Teds, and all us in between just kept it together right through the 1970s.

The ICF, they don't know that side of it; they've never taken a slap. We used to get away with it because the other firms showed us too much respect. And you knew, if you went in the North Bank at Arsenal, that it wasn't the right firm. You'd look around you and think, We could come unstuck here. But our rivals just used to fold on the name of West Ham. And those years when the right faces didn't go for whatever reason, we got away with murder really to be honest. If a certain face wasn't there, everyone used to panic. 'Oh no, Cass ain't here, Gardner's not here, Swallow's not here. What we gonna do?' But in the old days, you made do with what you had. Mile End had

Bugsy, the Coopers, and all that. And, if Bugsy didn't turn up, there were other people there, like Kaydee, to take the leadership on.

I remember Harry Cripps's testimonial in 1972. It was a Thursday night and Mile End Station was the meet. There were the usual Mile End suspects – Bugsy, Kaydee and that. I was with Stratford. There was the Andersons, Brownie – all the usual Stratford lot. At the time there were only two firms there at West Ham, and that was Mile End and Stratford. There was no such thing as Canning Town. Teddy Bunter's firm, I think, were just coming on to the scene. But it was mainly Mile End and Stratford. And Bugsy the one with the gold tooth walked round at Mile End Station and said, 'You can go, you can go, you can't go, you can't go, you can't go, you can go.' He actually went round to every single person there telling them whether they could go or not. And I thought, Who the fuck do you think you are to say, 'You can't go.'

And I looked at him and I thought, Now what the fuck do I do? And Brownie stepped forward and said I was with them. I remember Bill being there. He was in with the Mile End firm. He had his donkey jacket on. And I've never witnessed anything like it in my life. There were meat cleavers, axes, chains – everything. In the game, on the terraces. To be quite honest, I was absolutely shitting myself when I saw what Mile End took up there. I'm not a tool person. And inside the ground it just all kicked off and it was every man for himself, and I remember Bill then. I don't know if he had a chain or what he was using – maybe it was an iron bar because I know the crash barrier got ripped up. Millwall didn't do West Ham. West Ham didn't do Millwall. It was just going backwards and forwards. It was just all of us standing there, because it was a big crowd that night, and it was just actually toe-to-toe fighting. I've never seen anything like it since. Everyone got together outside and Millwall came out. Someone gave a shout and then it was back through the big main gates and we chased them all the way back up on to the terracing.

When we went to Stamford Bridge we used to go in the Shed every year. You paid through the turnstiles and you had a little forecourt and then you had the steps leading up to the Shed. And all Chelsea were standing at the top. And I went in with Gardner and his little firm – he had a name and a firm then – and they were all pointing. 'There's Gardner, there's Gardner,' and that's all they were really interested in. They all wanted Gardner. This was an early get-in to take the Shed. There weren't a lot of West Ham, and I sneaked off up the side and got up the stairs and I was actually standing up with Chelsea, and then all of a sudden he just started walking up the stairs and he actually clumped one of them. And then the rest of West Ham that were with him just surged up the stairs. But that's what I got from Gardner. His presence was awesome then; everyone knew it. And he didn't give a fuck. He just walked into this death trap and went, 'Fuck them.'

Then there was the time at Birmingham New Street when Wolves were playing Cardiff. Cardiff were on the platform and we turned up because we were waiting on the Zulus. I remember there were 150 West Ham and Cardiff must have had about the same numbers or they might have had a few more. I've got the utmost respect for Cardiff because I remember the old days when Stratford used to go over the Orient when they had Cardiff. Cardiff used to have big men. And Bill just went up to one of them and said, 'Get your toy army off the platform.' I couldn't believe Cardiff swallowed it, and they went. They disappeared. I mean the man must hold some sway for people not to even question him. Not one of them came back with, 'Well, who the fucking hell are you?' They all knew who he was and no one had the bottle.

BUNTER

I've known Bill about 35 years. What a lovely man, and he also has a lovely family. I've seen Bill in many rucks, such as Stoke in the semi-final in the 1970s; Man United in the Cup at Old Trafford against his old foe, Banana Bob; and on one cold evening in the 1970s against Stockport away. Bill wore a bright-orange boiler-suit. There was no more than 50–60 of us in their end. We were fighting Stockport and Man City fans who joined up together. We all stood our ground with Bill and Ted. It was me, Simmo and the rest of the TBF. The Old Bill didn't have a clue. Bill has been in many a ruck and taken a couple of clumps, but he gave more out against some of the top boys about – they know who they are.

I also remember when Bill's second wife got a clump at Sheffield United away. Bill went fucking mental. But I must say, Bill wasn't really in the TBF or any other firm, he was always on his own.

CARLISLE MALCOLM

All I can think about Bill is, to me, he's the Godfather of West Ham. I've been going to West Ham since I was eight years old and I'm now 45. I started going to away matches when I was 12, about 1972. One of my first away matches was Burnley. When the game had finished, me and my mate were crapping ourselves how to get back to the station and what trouble there would be. When it was about to kick off Bill saw that we were worried and he got a couple of the boys to take us back to the station. Ever since that game Bill has always looked out for me and made sure I was OK. Bill always looked after me, took me under his wing and I thank him for that. He is a good friend and always will be. And yes, you can say he is a legend among us Hammers fans, though I have never seen Bill in a bad scrap because I'm not much of a fighter myself.

LOL

West Ham were away to Sheffield United in 1973. As usual, we planned to travel to the game by train and, as usual, we went by InterCity and not on the smelly specials. During the week we'd heard several rumours regarding the 'notorious' Cockney Reds. The Cockney Reds had built up a reputation around the country and particularly in London. Apparently they thought they were the boys. The top dogs. They wreaked havoc everywhere they went. Then, as they returned home to London, they had some more with groups of returning London fans. We'd never really encountered the Reds, just heard about their escapades from fans of other clubs. It seemed that, every single time they returned home to London from a game, they never bumped into West Ham. That was something that always amused us. They said it was a coincidence, although we knew different.

The day we played Sheffield United, Manchester United were away to Birmingham. The story was that the Cockney Reds were going to hang around at New Street Station for our train. At the time the Cockney Reds were led by a bloke called Banana Bob. What kind of fucking name was that? My brother reckoned it was because he was a bit of a slippery bastard. We were to find out a bit later that it was more than likely because he was as yellow as a banana and his pants turned brown just as quickly as a banana skin. The game at Sheffield wasn't much to write home about. It was a boring 0–0 draw and we had a little bit of fun with the Shoreham Aggro.

Remember, all this was years before mobile phones and any information was spread by the rumour mill rather than hard evidence or actual contact. But we believed the rumour about the Cockney Reds and, more importantly, we'd heard the rumour about Banana Bob's apparent threat to do Bill Gardner on the train.

The train home had quite a few West Ham fans on it. There was no one special except for the last carriage which contained us. We were laughing and joking most of the way. Bill was his usual unassuming self, joining in and laughing at all the banter. When the train pulled in to New Street we noticed lots of red and white. Mancs! But the majority of them were normal fans returning home – men with kids and some anorak types. They were no threat and of no interest to us. The ones we were interested in were the Cockney Reds, if in fact they were there at all.

As the train pulled out it didn't take long for the whispers to get out that Banana Bob and his cronies were on board. This was what Bill had been waiting for. He got up and didn't ask if anyone was gonna join him. He headed off along the carriage and a good few of us followed him. He could handle anyone face to face. We just wanted to make sure no coward was gonna make a name for himself by coming at Bill from behind. We walked through every carriage and asked anyone we didn't recognise if they knew Banana Bob. To a man they all shook their heads. As we got further and further along the carriages we were getting more and more into Manc territory. We could see the fear and hatred in their eyes, although none would return eye contact for very long.

By the time we reached the last carriage the atmosphere was one of fear, excitement and anticipation. Was the fruit man here? Was it gonna go off? We were heavily outnumbered in terms of bodies, but with Bill Gardner up front you were never outnumbered.

Finally, in the last carriage, Bill announced, 'Good afternoon, chaps, I'm Bill Gardner, does anyone know where Banana Bob is?' Every non-West Ham eye looked to the corner. At last, the infamous Bee-nana Bob. Bill said, 'I understand you plan to do me, son. Well, here I am, how about it?' Banana mumbled something about it not being the right place or the right time. He said that, if he did Bill, then we'd all jump in. To be honest, if he had done Bill, I'd have been out of there like a shot because he would have had to be fucking Superman! Bill told Banana Bob that it would be one on one. None of us would join in if none of his cronies did. Remember, there were only about 10 of us as opposed to a carriage load of them. Again Bob bottled, telling Bill they'd get another chance.

Bill told Bob he could have the first punch and put his face up close to Bob's. Again the Manc bottled. Bill then took off his belt, a thick leather one with a great big buckle on it, and threw it to Bob. 'Go on,' he said, 'I'll let you use this.' Banana Bob bottled it for the last time. As he walked to the door, Bill told him, 'You're two bob, mate,' grabbed his belt and walked out.

We never heard from Banana Bob any more. The story of him bottling it big time spread through the right channels. The legend that was Bill Gardner moved on another significant step.

MOUTHY BILL

We were in Sheffield in the early 1980s – about the time you had to have passes to get on the football special. They had only just started to run these trains again after all the past troubles of teams smashing them up. Now they returned with this new system of issuing passes to the fans travelling on them. I never had a pass so someone I knew who wasn't going gave me his. So I just put my photo over his and travelled up on the special.

We got down the ground and into the game, and as you looked to your left there was a little alleyway leading down the other side of the barrier on to the pitch. I saw four West Ham supporters walking down it and a big mob of Sheffield United supporters following them down there. And, without thinking, I jumped over on to the pitch and ran into where it was going to go off. As I did it, Bill Gardner did it as well. I saw him run down on his own. I've gone in there and Old Bill have jumped in quite quick and stopped it. They nicked a bunch of us, and Bill Gardner's shouted 'steward'. But I was nicked, and they pulled me out and walked me round the pitch, marching me past the stands when all I could hear was, 'Nick him, officer, he's a fucking hooligan.' It was my pals Alfie, Martin, Terry and all them. 'He's always starting trouble, officer.'

That's the worst feeling in the world being nicked, and I had this lot abusing me for a laugh.

So it's all a bit of a process when you are nicked and after about half an hour this copper came in. He was rubbing his hands together and he went, 'That's it, you're in trouble now.'

I went, 'What's that?'

And he went, 'We'll take your pass away from you.'

No sooner had he'd said that than Bill Gardner walked in. He went, 'Right, get his pass. That's the last game he'll ever go to.' And he marched me out and I got away with a nicking!

I went, 'Cheers, Bill.'

And he said, 'No worries. Now I don't want to take you back into the ground, so make sure you fuck off,' giving me one of his winks.

KEVIS

It was Swansea City in 1981 and it was their big day. The Hammers were in town and they were unveiling their new stand. I was in the North Bank with my mates and we were sizing up potential apres-football entertainment. The match kicked off and it was the standard fare of anti-Cockney chants and singing. We were mooching around when all of a sudden we clocked 30–40 geezers in donkey jackets and sheepskins, filing through the Swansea ranks and lining up across the terrace. They were poker-faced and full of intent. These weren't Jacks; we knew that straight away. This was West Ham United infiltration. But who? It was too late now for thinking. This big bloke had just walked brazenly into their end with a firm of West Ham, signalling a start to hostilities. This was Gardner, my first and lasting memory of a West Ham United legend.

I met Bill in Scotland during a West Ham pre-season one year. We were both outside McDiarmid Park in Perth, home of St Johnstone. He was kicking a ball on the grass with our young boys. He'd obviously aged a bit, but the aura was still present. The man commands respect with his mere presence. We got chatting and he gave me his card. 'Gimme a call any time,' he said. 'I'll see you right with programmes, tickets, and so on,' and he has been true to his word ever since.

This man is so polite and respectful to my wife and young son, yet he's a feared man of violence – obviously a man of good old-fashioned morals who, away from the football, could be everyone's favourite uncle. These are my images of Bill, both the fighter and the gentleman. Bill Gardner: hooligan, or just a plain, decent, hard bastard who liked a row? I hope he doesn't get remembered as a hooligan.

JA

I got trapped and cornered by a lot of Millwall when getting the train out of Euston Station. I was with Gardner and Stanford that day. That would have been 1980/81. We used to go away a lot then on the InterCity train and we were going somewhere like Grimsby. I had to meet them all round a certain station at about eight-thirty in the morning, but because I'd been out partying I'd missed it. And I was coming into the station and everyone said, 'Oh you've missed them. Cass and all them have gone.' And they said, 'Bill's over there.'

And I went round and I saw Bill Gardner, and he said, 'Yeah, you've missed them, John, but you can stick with me because I might need some help here. Everyone's gone; it's just the club supporters' train with the normal club supporters on.'

So I was with him and all of a sudden we were just mobbed. We were just surrounded by all these people screening us. There were only two of us and a few other West Ham there, but they were making out they'd been told not to say anything, so they were keeping a low one. And we've got all these people round us and they've started giving us dirty looks. And Gardner was fronting them all. All of a sudden we've heard Leeds coming in off the train, and a load of these supporters around us have all steamed over and given Leeds a good hiding. And they've come back and a woman walked past and Gardner's gone, 'You want to look after your little kids otherwise they're all going to get a good hiding. They keep acting flash in front of just a couple of geezers.'

And the woman turned round and gave him a nasty look and said, 'They're not my boys.' Then under her jacket she showed us a Tottenham scarf. And she said, 'They're Millwall,' and obviously all the blokes who had just beaten up Leeds were Millwall. Of course, none of them had any scarves on and when they've heard that they've all started singing Millwall.

We thought they were Tottenham at first because none of them had any scarves on, and they were all round us. And Gardner's gone up to every single person and said, 'Come on then, if you're Millwall you've just given Leeds a hiding, what one of you has got the front to fucking start now?' And he's fronted every single one. He's walked round each one individually and not one of them said anything. There were just the two of us. I've never seen anyone do it.

And all the other West Ham were now on the fucking train. And I always remember there was Brian Blower, the club official in charge of the tickets for the away travel, and he ran and got on the train. There was a ginger fella there and, as soon as he heard the Millwall, he was off like a light. He was pretty hefty but I hadn't see him lose so much weight the way he sped that 20 metres, like, he was gone. There was other people there but obviously at the end of the day there's just three of us really who's doing it, all the others just disappeared. By this stage there was me, Gardner and Stanford, and all that Millwall firm have run to us and they've stopped about 10 foot away. And then Gardner said, 'Well, come on then,' he said, 'we don't need anyone else. There's three of us. Who's got the bottle?'

And then three of them have walked up and one's got a walking stick. And the feller's gone, 'Who's Gardner?'

And the three of us said, 'We're all Gardner.'

Give them their due, there were only three of them who came over and all their other mob just stood there. So there was us three and them three.

And then the fella with the walking stick said, 'No, I know Gardner.' And he whacked this other West Ham lad with the walking stick and punched him. And with that we've just whacked the Millwall supporters. The lad who got hit held his mouth. I whacked one and Gardner's whacked one. And with that, fucking all of the Millwall have chased us. So we've started running, but they ran about 10 yards and they stopped. And we just got on the train. And that was it.

But to see it when they were all round us was amazing. He fronted every single one of them and they all bottled it. He walked up to each one individually who was round us, all round the perimeter of that circle, and there were loads of them, and he offered each one out and not one of them said anything.

Afterwards on the train he just said, 'Yeah, give them a good hiding tonight, we'll catch up with all the others and get the others.'

But being with him, even though we were outnumbered, I think they were more scared than us. At the end of the day, he was the top man and he'd always give his due, and I never saw him get a hiding. That kind of presence, it just gives you the feeling that you were going to beat them. Even though there were just three of us and all the other West Ham weren't going to help us. When he said he might need a hand, I said, 'Yeah, OK,' as I thought there were loads of other West Ham, but then I saw them all reading, and it wasn't porno mags like the ICF would read. They were all reading the fucking *Times* or the *Guardian* and papers like that, with their packed lunches. It would have been different if Bill wasn't there, we would probably have got quite a hiding. But with his name and his presence, he just shit them all up.

CHESTERFIELD MICK

It was Stoke away in the 1980s and I travelled to London on the Friday night and stayed at Manor Park at a West Ham mate's flat. We all met on the Saturday morning and travelled to Stoke from London. Bill was on the train, as were one or two other West Ham big names. Vaughny was up to his usual tricks selling scratch cards – funny, but I never had a single winner.

On arrival at Stoke there was a heavy police presence, which was usual for West Ham being in town. As we came out of the station, about 15 or 20 of us started to drift away from the pack. I was with Vaughny, Swallow, my mate from Manor Park and Bill Gardner, and we made our way up to the ground and, without it ever being discussed, went round to Stoke's end. In single file and as if we had never met before we went into the ground. We all stood just behind the goal, about three-quarters of the way down the terrace. My next memory is Bill saying he was going to get a drink. He had only been gone a couple of minutes when it happened.

Word must have got around West Ham were on their end. In truth, it was only a matter of time before it went off. A good mob of Stoke had come from the front and steamed into us. We held our own but were outnumbered.

As the violence quelled slightly, with stewards and Old Bill coming from nowhere, I looked to the left in the direction that Bill Gardner had gone. I could see Bill making his way back taking on all who got in his way. It was like a scene from an old Buster Keaton film as Bill made his way through, taking on anyone who opposed him, never once taking a step back. West Ham had made their mark in Stoke.

Another time I remember was Nottingham Forest away in the 1980s. We arrived at two o'clock in Nottingham, which was late for me. I made my way up to the City Ground and went into the stand next to the away end. When I got in there I saw Bill Gardner sat with Lewisham and a few others. As I went up to speak to Bill, I noticed he had two black eyes. He explained he'd been jumped from behind near the station, but the Forest fans had run away. Bill explained to me that he was too old to go chasing those northern cunts around the streets of Nottingham. Just behind us in the ground Schobie and a few other older West Ham blokes were sat, and instead of singing for their team they all proceeded to sing, 'Two lovely black eyes, he's got two lovely black eyes,' which Bill and all the other West Ham fans in that end thought was hilarious. One thing Bill Gardner isn't short of is a sense of humour. That same day it went off at half-time as West Ham, led by Bill Gardner, steamed into the Forest boys who were no match for him, even wounded.

Another time I remember was at Aberdeen in a pre-season friendly in 1980/81. West Ham had a mob of about 90 for the Aberdeen tour. Man United were up there so it was bound to be naughty. Once again, Bill was ever present. There had been various skirmishes during the stay, but on the last day we had all made our way back to the hotel and were sat relaxing, talking about the game, when McGrath and some other geezer who had stopped for something to eat came running into the bar and told us that Man United were on their way in big numbers. Bill stood up, with a certain aura that always surrounded him, and we all made our way outside. The Old Bill had tried to keep us apart. Bill and a few of the others made their way through and steamed in. Once again, Bill was like a colossus, leading the small mob of West Ham boys forward. West Ham were outnumbered but the Mancs were outclassed. As Bill went forward the Mancs backed off. Another result for West Ham.

Bill once told me that when he is in the company of undercover police he gets an uncontrollable cough. Once, when on holiday with family, they got in conversation with another family on the beach. Bill started to cough and told his partner he thought the bloke was Old Bill. True to Bill's instincts, later on in the conversation the bloke revealed he was Old Bill.

Having supported West Ham all my life and followed

them for 26 years, I have met various types of people on my journey. Many come and go and many are charlatans. I am not a man easily fooled, neither do I have a void in my life or am the sort of person looking for a hero figure. But, having spent time in the company of Bill Gardner over the years, you realise that there is much more to Bill Gardner than the terrace legend: there is Bill Gardner the West Ham fan, the man who travels up and down the country, week in, week out, to watch his team; Bill Gardner the family man, who spends time with his children pursuing their footballing dream; and also Bill Gardner the friend. Although a man of few words, Bill would always have time for his friends and fellow supporters. On many occasions Bill has got me tickets for certain big games and always the tickets come at the cost that Bill pays – he's never a man to gain on a friend.

To sum Bill up, the only word that keeps coming to mind is legend.

DENNIS

I've been going to football since the early 1970s. That's over three decades. One of the best things about going to football is the people you meet, and I have made some great mates over the years. And Bill Gardner certainly comes into that category. I first knew who Bill was when I was a kid of 13 or 14. It was at an away game at Turf Moor, Burnley's ground. The West Ham fans were in a big side terrace enclosure and the main bulk of West Ham fans were bunched in the middle. I was standing on the edge of the bunch so I could get a better view of the game. The next thing I knew, a mob of 100–150 Burnley fans came flying in, punching and kicking anyone in sight. I know with the age I was I was really scared. The next thing I saw was Bill and Big Ted in front of 30 or 40 of West Ham's top boys coming through. The Burnley fans realised what they were up against and backed off big time.

I remember Bill saying to me, 'Are you OK, son? Come and stand over here with us.' That made me feel safe, and from that day on Bill was always someone I have looked up to, and I know over the years there are many people that go to football who have had similar experiences where Bill has helped them out.

I really started to know Bill properly the day after we beat Arsenal to win the FA Cup in 1980 – what a great day that was. We were right outside the main gates of the East Ham town hall celebrating with thousands of other West Ham fans when the team brought the FA Cup back to the East End. Bill's late mum, his ex-wife and his daughter were all there celebrating with a very proud Bill that day.

The next season we were in Europe in the first round of the European Cup Winners' Cup. We played Castilla in Madrid's Bernabeu stadium in Spain. There was a lot of trouble that night and a young West Ham fan, Frank Saint from Stepney, lost his life by being run down by a coach. The West Ham supporters were blamed for the trouble. Bill was very upset by this and put himself out to be interviewed by various papers to try and put the record straight, but unfortunately Frank Saint's family never got the justice they deserved.

In the next round we went to Romania. There was no official trip run by the club, fearing there would be further trouble and the club would be kicked out of Europe, so we went with a tour firm called Trans Euro Travel, who were based in the West End of London. Bill got on well with the company boss, Mike Ross, and he helped to organise the trip, making sure all the right people knew about it. I remember this game well and at the final whistle the Romanians started to throw bottles and bricks at us. We were in a small group behind the goal. Bill just said, 'If we retaliate, we will get the blame and we will be kicked out of Europe.'

Bill got everyone to stand their ground and not get provoked. In the end the Romanian police brought a water cannon in, although they didn't need to use it because the crowd dispersed. I think West Ham United Football Club owed Bill a big thank you that day for getting everyone to keep their cool. UEFA had made it quite clear that, if there was any trouble involving West Ham fans, the club would be slung out of the competition.

Back to the domestic scene. I was working with Bill on the Irons Travel Club, which was the official travel club organised by West Ham United for fans to travel to away games. The four years that I worked with Bill stewarding on the trains I can honestly say there was never any trouble with anyone because everyone knew Bill and had total respect for him. Bill was everyone's mate, and everyone was Bill's mate, and that's just the way it was. I remember during that period we were at an away game, I think it was at Leicester, when a fight broke out and a policeman was getting a kicking from a group of Leicester fans. Whatever you think of the Old Bill, one man getting kicked and punched by a group can't be right. Bill had the bottle to go and help him and he actually got a letter of thanks from the Chief Constable thanking him for his actions. Mind you, Bill did knock the arse out of it. He used to take it everywhere with him. If there was any trouble and Bill got grabbed by the Old Bill, he would show them the letter and get away with it. I think Bill got that letter out more times than Sam Fox got her tits out in those days.

I am now in my forties and I have travelled with Bill hundreds of times up and down the country over the years. I class Bill as a very close mate. I have always enjoyed his company and we have had some great football debates over the last 30 years. Bill to me is the ultimate West Ham fan. I still have the same amount of respect for Bill now as I did all those years ago when I was that frightened teenager that he pulled to safety at Burnley. To me, Bill really is West Ham's number one.

GARY FIRMAGER

The story of Bill and the way he was treated by the club has been interpreted in many different ways, but I have to hold my hands up to one thing, and that was elongating Bill's absence from the ground. Well, for another couple of weeks, anyway.

I had been championing Bill's cause for a number of years in my fanzine *Over Land And Sea*, and I just couldn't understand the logic in Bill coming to each and every home game, dropping his son off, who then went into the game, waiting around, and then them going home together afterwards, because of the existence of a lifelong ban. A ban that was, I felt, really unfair and unjust as it was issued and left in place after Bill's arrest, for which he was later acquitted of any wrongdoing in what was a showcase trial.

At the time, I was having a number of meetings with the club managing director Peter Storrie, who I felt was a real breath of fresh air at the club. He was a man who took a great deal of interest in what the fans thought and went out of his way to listen to various groups. In fact, during the notorious Hammers Bond Scheme days, Peter Storrie had the bottle not only to attend, but also to stand on a chair in The Denmark Arms pub and address an extremely hostile 300–400 Hammers fans who were more interested in lynching him than listening to him. Bottle like that deserves respect, and from that day onwards I had a very good working relationship with Mr Storrie.

He wasn't anti-fanzine, as most clubs' MDs were, and would listen. After the Bond Scheme demonstrations had gone (another significant victory for fan power), meetings between the fanzine and Peter Storrie continued on a regular basis. We used to meet up and discuss just about anything and everything. And it wasn't always like old pals, either. If there was something to be said, it was. By either party. And as often as we would be able to discuss something, we'd also disagree vehemently with each other about something else.

But Peter Storrie did try to understand the workings of the West Ham fans and took the club a long way forward in many aspects. Indeed, racism at football, and specifically Upton Park, was something that we discussed and that we acted on together – club and fanzine working side by side. One thing remained constant, though, through every meeting – allowing Bill Gardner back into the ground and putting an end to his lifetime ban.

At first Peter Storrie was really interested in listening, but over time it became clear that he wasn't in total control of the situation and that he was being heavily influenced by others at the club. At the same time I understood that Bill had been having the odd conversation with Storrie as well, and the two men got along OK. It was perhaps only surface deep, but even that was a start.

As time went by, I felt as though Storrie really wanted to allow Bill back into the ground, but just felt his hands were tied. The time had come to bite the bullet and make a show. In *Over Land and Sea* I did just that. I put the offer on the table of £10,000, payable instantly at the first sign of trouble from Bill over the first season they let him back in. They could reinstate the lifelong ban and give the money to charity. It was a bold gesture and I can reveal a bullshit one too. Ten fucking grand? I didn't have money like that and I wouldn't have paid up either.

But it was a way of getting maximum publicity for Bill. And it stirred up a lot of attention. The fanzine was selling like hot cakes; everyone wanted to know if the current issue was the one with the '10 grand Bill money offer'. It wasn't about selling more fanzines; it was about getting Billy back inside the ground. And anyway, I knew Billy well enough to know that, even if I had got the money to start with, it would have stayed safely in my offshore bank account!

Bill didn't want anything more than to take his boy to West Ham – a family tradition – and I wanted to help. Then it all went tits up. A few days after the article came out I had a very angry Peter Storrie on my answerphone, asking if I could come in for a meeting. This I did. When I got there the pleasantries of previous meetings were not exchanged. Storrie had a copy of *OLAS* on the table, marked at the page where my 10 grand show of bravado shone from the glossy black and white pages.

I can't remember word for word what he said, but it was something like, 'What the fuck is this all about? What a load of cobblers.'

I explained that it was my way of putting my trust in Bill, and the club couldn't lose. Couldn't lose at all.

Then Storrie sat down and explained that after the continued discussions with me about Bill he had decided finally to act and do the decent thing and bring Billy back into the fold. Because I had given it the big one, he said West Ham would now have to hold back their offer to Bill, or it would have made it look as though the fans had won another war with the club. And, coming so quickly after the Bond Scheme, that couldn't be seen to be done. I was gutted. I rang Bill and explained, but he just laughed. It was no big deal – another few weeks didn't matter.

It was a satisfactory end to it all and I think Peter Storrie should be credited for many things. But the main one for me, and of course Bill and his family, is using a bit of common sense and letting an absolutely dedicated West Ham fan back among his own.

Storrie phoned me up on the eve of Bill's return and told me that Bill would be allowed in the next day. I was delighted with the news. A little bit of small talk followed before he came out with, 'Ten grand, you never had 10 grand anyway, did you?'

'Of course I fucking haven't,' I laughed. 'And, even if I did, I wouldn't give it to you lot of thieving bastards…'

GRANT

I will never forget sitting in a Russian hotel breakfast room after West Ham played Dynamo Tbilisi. Everyone was blanking us and waiting for Bill to come marching over to us to ask, 'What was all that about smashing the room up?' It's one of those things when you go somewhere and everyone tells you not to do something – not there, because that's not the place to misbehave. Well, what do you do? Of course you're going to do it, aren't you? If someone had said, 'I'm going to have a right old tear-up,' we probably wouldn't have bothered. There was me, Andy, Turner and a couple of others including a mate of mine from Benfleet, who became a bit of a patsy.

We went out with him the night before the game and he ended up getting a bit drunk, as always. So he came into our room and messed himself up. And he was sick down our curtains. So we said tomorrow we'd have the party in his room, all joking, but it obviously gathered momentum.

And during the next day we've gone in the supermarket, took one of the trolleys, filled it up absolutely to the brim and paid for it. We filled the bath with cold water, put all the beers and wine in it, and after the match went back to his room. 'Yeah, tonight we're going to smash your room up,' we said to this feller.

All of a sudden there was a shout. You saw this jet of water fly out of the toilet. He was in there, and he'd pulled the cistern off. Once that started I remember there were a couple of books by the bed that went off the balcony. And then it was just like a free for all. We were like tearing up the mattresses and everything; there was nothing left in the room. Everything went. You could say it was a bit rock 'n' roll. The telly would have gone, but there wasn't one.

There was a garden at the bottom of the hotel, but we didn't even look where it was landing. We were on the 11th floor. So the place was flooding at one end, and we've got all this wine going all over the place. We've gone back to our room and within an hour there's bang, bang, bang, 'policia' and all that. Now the funniest thing is that the bloke that this fella was supposed to be sharing with was one of Wickford's mates – a pure pisshead. In Moscow where we stayed first of all we found him by the lift – he never made it to the room. And the same thing in Tbilisi, he never made it to the room, but, when the names have come up on the register, they've got my mate and they've got this fella.

We've gone down to breakfast, sort of sheepish, not saying anything. Everyone knew we were the outcasts. So we were sat at the table and everyone's looking over because they've been told not to do anything in Russia whatever you do. Well, to break the ice, Bill came over to the table, and he's gone, 'I've seen a lot of things in my time but you fucking lot have taken the piss. You're bang out of order.'

And then it turned out they've got the fella, our mate, and obviously we realised that we were responsible for it as much as anyone, so we were saying we weren't gonna leave without him. The best bit about it was they collared the other bloke, the drunk, and he sat in the room all coated in beer. And then the representative from West Ham was going, 'Well you've done this, you've smashed this, you've done that.'

And the fella who hadn't even been in his room has turned to my mate and gone, 'I weren't that drunk, was I?'

So in the end we had a whip round, because even at that time it was a lot of money. There was £1,000 of damage, and in Russia in 1980 £1,000 was serious money. So we had a whip round and we just so happened to have a bit over the top, so we had a share out. The old Russians couldn't make it out because no one misbehaves in Russia. That was the thing, though, they shouldn't have told us that in the first place.

BOATSY AND WILMOT [FOREST]

BOATSY: It was about 1982. The Cockneys caught the train about 50-handed and we knew they were coming. Me and all the Forest lads came up and we stood on the corner railings. They spread out across the whole road, but there weren't that many of them. Bill was at the front and he had a three-quarter-length beige duffle coat on. He had curly hair at the time. And he spread his arms out wide like a flying condor. And he went, 'Come on,' like that. And Forest just went backwards, backwards, backwards. They didn't say nothing.

WILMOT: They didn't charge us; they just kept walking.

BOATSY: They just walked us, and we kept going backwards, backwards. And I thought, Fuck this. The whole Forest lot bottled it. I'm not being funny. I looked up to the old ones, and nobody was doing nothing, and I thought,

Fuck this. I was about 17 and this Bill Gardner was built like a double-decker bus. I was game as fuck, and nobody did nothing. They walked us from the Bentinck Hotel all the way down to Redmayne and Todds Sports Shop.

WILMOT: Bill Gardner was in the middle of the road and he was massive.

BOATSY: He didn't make any noise, he just did that with his arms, and they were all round him. And he didn't give a fuck. He kept going like that all the way down the fucking road. That was the first time I'd seen West Ham and I thought, They're fucking evil. You don't fuck with the fucking mad.

WILMOT: The thing is, we hadn't seen that kind of action. We hadn't seen that presence, that coolness. We hadn't seen it before.

BOATSY: They were cool as fuck.

WILMOT: No screaming, no shouting 'come on, let's have it'. They just walked right up to us. I'd never seen it before.

BOATSY: I was the last to back off and I was only a kid and I thought, I ain't fucking doing it. Fuck it. That was it. Forest ran. They just disintegrated. I've got to admit it. They were the best I've seen. That's why I always rate West Ham. In those days as well they didn't give a fuck. Forest were no mugs. We'd done everything since I'd been going, and that was the best fucking firm – the presence of Bill was amazing. I fucking knew who he was. Two years later the whole lot went: bottles, bricks, the lot. West Ham just stood their ground in the middle of that old garage forecourt. There were only 20 West Ham surrounded by 200 Forest. I didn't realise it was Bill Gardner and that. I was inside at the time. But a lot of teams would say you would have to have a tank with you to have a go at West Ham. That's what I heard on the grapevine.

WILMOT: Coming across Trent Bridge and he was at the front and NC obviously knew who he was. One of our old lads obviously spotted him coming across Trent Bridge, and the police were all round the West Ham. But there were only about 50 of them and this lad sort of just leaned in and swung a punch at him because it was him. And he was telling us all later that he swung one at Bill Gardner. It was that big a deal.

SCHOBIE

When I was asked to write about Bill I thought that it would be a simple thing to do, as all I would have to do is write down about all the good and bad times that I have had with him. But after some thought I found it wasn't that simple and to most people it would be boring as you had to be there, as the saying goes. I asked Bill if I could tell any story I wanted to and his reply was, 'Within reason.'

One particular story about Bill that always brings a smile to me and my brother Lol's face was when the Brothers Grim, as Bill calls us, decided to put chilli flakes into a large packet of nuts and raisins. We were stood in the Chicken Run, and Bill, the greedy git that he was, asked if he could have some. Lol straight away said, 'You can have the lot, mate. We don't want any more.'

With this, Bill chomped down a couple of handfuls of nuts and after about two minutes his bonce was as red as a beetroot and he had steam coming out of every orifice. Me and Lol had to watch our steps for a good few weeks and to this day Bill will never take a bit of tucker off me unless I try it first.

Food is one of his favourite things and there's another story to do with that. We were out in Romania for the Cup Winners' Cup and I was sharing a room with him. Bill's arse was making buttons to get down to the restaurant for dinner. 'Come on, Schobie, I'm fucking starving,' he said. 'Let's go and have some sustenance.' So off the two of us went down to the restaurant for our meal.

'I don't like the look of this grub, Bill,' I said, 'what do you reckon this meat is?'

'Don't matter what it is, just get it down your neck,' said Bill, but I wasn't having it and was just eating the veg. This gave Bill the hump, as he doesn't like to see food wasted. 'You make me laugh,' he said, 'eat the fucking stuff.'

I still wasn't having it, so Bill decided he was going to ask the waiter what the meat was.

'Oi, John, over here. What meat is this?' he said. I thought it was a pointless question as the waiter didn't understand a single word of English. 'This meat, what is it?' Bill asked again.

'Look, forget it, Bill, I don't want the meat,' I said.

Then Bill piped up with his all-time classic. 'Listen, John, this meat,' he said, pointing at it with his knife, 'is it moo?'

The waiter shook his head.

'Well, is it baa?'

Again, the water shook his head.

'Well, what the fuck is it then?' he said.

With this, the waiter just went 'woof' and walked away. I jumped away from the table and shot off to the bog to chuck up, but when I got back the meat had gone off my plate and was on Bill's!

'You dirty bastard,' I said, 'how can you eat that?'

Bill just looked at me and said, 'If you're hungry, you'll eat anything.'

When we got home I tried to get a licence so he could piss up lampposts.

In Sarah, James and Danny he has himself a fantastic family. I have seen the kids grow up and you wouldn't want for two more polite young men than them two, and that is to Bill and Sarah's credit. In young Danny you have the world's most compulsive giggler and he is always up for a titter or two when I occasionally drop my guts. I have known Bill for a long, long time and over the years things have changed, but not so our friendship.

TONBRIDGE CLIFF

The thing with Bill is that he's not like the football hooligan you know. I never thought of him as a football hooligan. I didn't see him like that. I always thought he was just a bloke who wanted to go and watch his team and he didn't want to take a backward step along the way. And, if you remember the 1970s and 1980s, it was a time when, if you wanted to go and watch a team, there were quite a lot of people that would stop you doing that.

There was a Youth Cup game at Millwall in the early 1980s when we all met at Mile End. There were maybe 100, no more than that. Swallow and Scully and people like that were there. We were on the train, and as we were coming down from Mile End to Whitechapel this Millwall chap got on and some West Ham youngsters hit him. And I remember Bill grabbing hold of the West Ham bloke and saying, 'Hang on, what's your game? West Ham don't go on like that.'

And immediately the bloke stopped, but the Millwall bloke was still stuck on the train with us, because obviously he couldn't get off. He was probably shitting himself knowing he was on a train with West Ham. But Bill had stopped him getting a good hiding. I still remember Bill saying to the West Ham lad, 'I'll be looking out for you when we get off the other end when we bump into their firm.' The youngster went quiet. But this shows you what Bill is like. He wasn't going to stand there and watch this one Millwall bloke get a good hiding off some youngster. Most will agree it's just not on, not if you're West Ham it ain't.

And it did go off when we actually got off the train at New Cross. We'd gone round the back, avoiding the main road, and come up through some park where we bumped into their mob. It went off a little bit and I don't know what happened to that West Ham bloke. He probably disintegrated into the background.

I remember some time in the early-80s up in Middlesbrough. I think we beat Boro and I know Paul Goddard scored two. Afterwards we were walking through the precinct and it really went off. It was a massive great row. Bill was there and I suppose there must have been 100–150 of us that got out of the escort after the game. We'd all just carried on walking and walking and Boro have some right big lumps. There was a lot of hand-to-hand fighting. The worst thing was they had got in behind us. I was with Ted and a few others right at the back being confronted by some big Boro blokes. I can remember Ted called to Bill, 'Look, it's over here.' Because people were running forward and as a unit we were getting stretched all over the place. Then all of a sudden Bill came to the back and he just went up to them and said something like, 'My name's Gardner.' And no sooner had he said that than it was like they just melted away.

I don't know whether they had heard of him or what, because there were some right lumps among them. I look at it as one of those defining moments. I mean, don't get me wrong, we were all confident and I don't think anyone thought they were ever going to get done, because quite simply there was nowhere for us to go. We had to get to the station and we had them at the sides of us and coming from behind. There were rocks coming over us. If we had got done, it would only have been if it had come on top for us proper. Quite simply, we had nowhere to run. There were a lot more of them than there were of us, but we had some right good people. We had people like Harrison, Swallow and Wildman. But it was just that moment where we were at the back and it was looking a little bit naughty. But Bill came over and then the row carried on somewhere else.

He just gives you the confidence. You see him there and you think, He ain't going to run; I'll stick with him. You have to wonder where people like that get that amount of confidence from. They've got to be special people to give you that sort of confidence. I mean, how often would you walk down the road with just a dozen of you when there's about 100 blokes waiting to do you? It's just not a sensible move, is it? But he did it time and time again and we've hardly ever come unstuck. I mean, I've got a few right-handers over the years, but I haven't been badly hurt or anything. You come out of these scraps unscathed and that just gives you the confidence to do it somewhere else. Sometimes having Bill's presence made you feel invincible. It made you feel, we're West Ham, and we've only got to go boo and you lot will run.

BONZO [NORWICH]

For Chelsea away in September 1984 we all met at Bethnal Green early doors, and what a mob we had. It was awesome in numbers and faces. After a short while Bill gave the shout like the general he was and off we went. We bowled off the tube at Sloane Square like an army in every way: we had the numbers, the excitement and to top it all the knowledge to give Chelsea a sound spanking. Up the King's Road we went with the surprise of being early and also with the firm to destroy these Home County wankers.

After walking all the way from Sloane Square we were now right on their manor and in the back streets of West London, when we all of a sudden met a hail of milk bottles. Chelsea were also about early and had stumbled on a milk float, which was their tool to try and back West Ham off their patch. Well, the bottles seemed to come flying over at us for ever, but the milk float soon emptied and Chelsea were gone as we made our way towards them. If my memory is correct, we then plotted up in a couple of pubs and took major liberties all day. Chelsea will tell it different but they always did, didn't they?

In the League Cup of 1983/84, West Ham were drawn against Bury in the first round, which was a two-legged affair. We played up there first and me and a couple of mates, Martin also from Norwich and Kevin from Bury St Edmunds, drove up in Martin's battered old Marina. We parked up near the bus station and then met up with Paul from Northampton, who was at that time my closest mate in the football scene. After a few beers in one of the local boozers, about 50 of us made our way to the ground and a few skirmishes occurred outside Gigg Lane. These were the early days of mobs going in the seats and in the Main Stand. We didn't have huge numbers, but then again we always knew everyone and knew we would back each other up.

Just before kick-off it went off in the side opposite where we were sitting. Harris had taken a small mob in there and the rumour was there were Mancs in there. Well, it seemed to go on for ages, but Old Bill eventually moved West Ham out and it quietened down. I think we won 2–1 and outside we had it right off and Bill took charge of us as we came under attack from all sides. Without someone with his bottle, we would have been in trouble, but he as always took the bull by the horns and into them we went. It was chaos and there was fighting all night in the back streets of Bury. We ended up at it all the way to the bus station and I can still see Bill now keeping us all together in a tight mob, and these were the days of the Old Bill being a bit slow to the scene.

Eventually they appeared, but by this time we had gone back towards the ground. We had parked near the bus station, so Bill made everyone, including Old Bill, go back towards the bus station so the three of us could safely get to our car. And that's the sort of thing Bill would do without thinking, even though he then had to go all the way to the other side of Bury.

VAUGHNY

I first heard of Bill Gardner when I was 14 years old. When West Ham were away on a Saturday, I used to watch my local team Southend United play on a Friday night and I would listen to the older ones talking about him. The first time I set eyes on him was at Middlesbrough in 1974. I said to Light and Bitter, a mate of mine, at the end of the game, 'What's everyone waiting for?'

He said, 'When Bill Gardner moves, all our firm will move.'

We waited for about 10 minutes and then he moved and all 250 West Ham moved as well. It was an unbelievable moment. Outside the ground he was leading the firm. There was a non-stop barrage of bricks, but he just kept going forward.

Over the years I got to become really good mates with Bill and can recall many battles with him. Like Derby County away, 1983/84, which was a night match. There were two minibuses of us and I was driving one of them. At the end of the game we came out of the ground and turned in the opposite direction to all the other West Ham as our van was parked in a different place to the coaches.

As we turned a corner there was a massive firm of Derby. Straight away they sussed us out and steamed into us.

There was a corner shop nearby and we gathered up in the doorway. There was a good firm of us – Light and Bitter, Giant, Shane, Cliff, Meatball, Big Ted. Their firm started coming at us and they had blokes throwing kung-fu kicks at us. I remember that Schobie shouted to Bill that our firm was going to run and I told him no one was going nowhere. Again and again Bill and Ted led us in, repeatedly driving them back and doing the blokes who were doing the kung-fu kicks. This battle went on for 15 minutes before mounted police came and broke it up. When the police escorted us back to the vans they could not believe it, as there were only 21 of us.

Then there was Man United away in maybe 1983/84. After getting to Manchester about noon there was a huge row in Argyle Square. In the end the police broke it up and put everyone on buses. We held back for the last bus and there were only enough of us to fill the top of a double-decker. When we got to the ground the Old Bill forgot all about us. As we crossed the crossroads there was a large firm of them to our left. I heard one of the Mancs shout out, 'Gardner, Gardner, I know you.' With that, they steamed into us, we steamed into them and they backed off.

A copper came along on a horse and said, 'Who are you?'

Bono, who was with us, said, 'Cockney Reds.'

So the copper said, 'Get on your way to the ground and keep moving.'

By then the mob on the other side of the road were

following us and we were having running battles with them. As we got to the bridge by the ground, Sammy the Engine turned up with a couple of hundred Mancs. They were coming at us from the opposite side of the road, behind us and in front of us. We had our backs to the railway bridge wall and we were holding our own. Bill was controlling the firm as usual. A copper's horse stuck itself between the two mobs until more coppers arrived and got us out of that one.

It's easy for me to sum up Bill. Bill had been going with the firm for three decades and took over from Joey Williams. There was not a leader anywhere in the country that had been the top man in a firm for that long, and never will be. When you were with him you always felt confident, no matter how heavily outnumbered you were. The firm I went with would never run in front of him, as we could never look him in the eye again, even though he would never hold it against people who ran. He was one of the nicest people you could meet and he had a great brain in a battle. Andy Swallow said to me years later that Bill Gardner was special because he could always hold the firm together. Sometimes that was the difference between winning and losing a ruck.

QPR DANNY AND JOHN [WOODHATCH FC]

DANNY: West Ham had Man United at home Bank Holiday Monday. There was John, me, Bill and Sarah, his missus. This was a live Sunday match and would have been mid-80s. Bill had a broken leg from playing football. We'd played football in the morning and driven up for a late-afternoon kick-off. Bill bought us tickets to get in. So, whatever the score was, after the match Bill had to wait for everyone to go because of his leg. He had to wait for everyone to clear. John went and got the car and we've walked out through the main entrance and all the West Ham supporters have gone.

Man United's main mob came walking up the road in an escort. They saw Bill and shouted out, 'Oh, look, the famous Billy Gardner. Fucking cripple,' and all that, giving him loads of abuse.

And he's just fucking spun and said, 'Come on, then.' He slammed down his crutches and said, 'All of you, now.'

And John saw it and came running over. 'Bill, Bill, no, no.'

And Bill's gone, 'John, get in the fucking car, this is down to me.' And he wouldn't have it.

And they all just fucking whimpered away. They didn't say no more after that. He shut them right up. And he wouldn't have any help when these Mancs decided to give it the large one. They were a little mob of about 40. There were police round them. But he wasn't asking for any help. That is the man. He can turn any situation around in literally minutes, can't he? When it's right on top he becomes the coolest man there. He never loses his bottle.

JOHN: We played for Woodhatch, Bill's team, that played in the Redhill District Sunday League, Division One. We were all looking forward to our first ever tour as a team. It was to be an end of season tour to Belgium. We were the first representatives from England to do with football to represent this country in Belgium after the Heysel Stadium tragedy. And we actually got a letter from the FA saying that.

There was a pub called The Knob that was run by a geezer that some of the people knew. We stayed in his pub and outside there was a golf course, and Bill Boy, Stanford, Ted Bunter, Porky Pat, all that lot all came on our football tour. We were 50-odd-handed in the boozer with the team and all the boys plus a few birds, and we all kipped in the pub and got on the coach and just drove off. But the thing I remember was outside the pub there was a little nine-hole golf course, literally across the road. The coach was parked up this little road next to where the pub was and a geezer in a mini had blocked us in. So we were trying to leave at six in the morning, and we were knocking on people's doors to find out whose car it was, but we couldn't find anyone.

So what we did was we picked the car up and put it on a green in the middle of a golf course. So he'd get up in the morning and find his fucking mini is sitting on the golf green. And then we got on the coach and went.

DANNY: We stayed in Ostend and it kicked right off. It was mental. In this ferry-port town they had a main square, like all these places do, and Vaughny and Ted and all that lot were all there. This main square had some cafes, and in one of the boozers there were a load of bikers. It was all the local Dutch herberts. We'd seen them earlier, but now it was the end of the night, four or five in the morning, and we were walking back and these bikers came over. One of them had a crash helmet and there was a bit of an altercation. Duncan, who plays for our team, he's taken a crash helmet over the head and it knocked him sparko. So this is what sparked it all off. There was the same number of us as there was of them, but after that it's become 20 on 20, because we've gone and got people and it was a running battle. It's gone off big time. The Old Bill came and we all got out without being nicked, but we got our own back on the bikers. The boys seriously fucking gave it to them. And Vaughny, Ted and half the West Ham lot that came out with us all fucked off the next day because they thought they'd killed one of the geezers.

The reality was nobody got killed, which was a relief because we went down the town the next night and the place was empty. It was like a ghost town, like the Wild West. Everywhere we walked past – they had all these strip clubs and that sort of thing there – and every time we walked past one of them, they shut the doors with their hands in their pockets. Everywhere we went they just nodded, like they knew who we were and what happened last night. We'd had a meeting first thing that morning where we'd said no one was to go out on their own, the whole town was fucking after us. We're the little mob that'd just done the main firm. Obviously these bikers must be something in Ostend. But two of them had been severely hospitalised.

JOHN: The other problem we had was we got out there and no one would play us. All the teams had been warned. You have to pass these tours with the FA. They said we can go out there as the tour had been pre-booked, but they didn't want us to play football. So all our games were cancelled. This was because of Heysel, so it was just unfortunate the timing of our football team tour.

So half of us have carried on, as the trip was

all paid for, and a few nights on we had a silly night. We had gone back to the hotel. Stanford and all that were there. We had a muck-about row in the hotel. It's all gone mental and got out of hand. The other lot have let all the fire extinguishers off, and they're like powder fire extinguishers, and basically the whole hotel was covered with a layer of dust. They were after me with these fire extinguishers. So what I did, because I was so knackered and drunk, I pushed the double wardrobe in front of my bedroom door. Unbeknown to me the old bird who owns the hotel has woken up in the morning and seen the whole hotel's been trashed, dust everywhere, and called the police. And the police knew that we'd been at it in the town centre.

They came into the hotel and I was still fast akip. And you know when you double take – all I remember is them banging on the door, and people trying to get in, and I'm going, 'Fuck off, you cunts,' because I thought it was our lot still trying to get in with these fire extinguishers, and I was still half-asleep. Basically, my door gets fucking kicked in and the next thing I know I'm lying in bed with fucking guns pointed at my temple. And I know Bill wasn't amused and he thought it was all down to me. I had to convince him it was Stanford and that lot.

They took all our passports, they took the whole team, and they gave us two hours to tidy up the whole hotel. They had armed police outside the hotel and they'd blocked the whole fucking road off. They took all our passports and gave us two hours to clear the hotel and fuck off out the country. And that was only down to Bill bartering. We were in jail, but Bill got us out. He's a diplomat. You know Bill. First of all he's sweetened up the hotel owner with a few readies, saying don't go too large on it. So then they talked to the Old Bill and said if the lads cleaned up the hotel and sorted it all they'd forgive them. They gave us a police escort to the border and back to the ferry to get us out.

JOHN: When I got banned from playing football, we went down to the meeting in front of the Surrey FA, and they banned me for a year, which was totally out of order. And Bill stood up as my representative and he stood up and put his briefcase on the table and said that he was willing to offer X-amount of money – £1,000 or £100,000 – it was a ridiculous load of money for the poxy league that we're in. Bill's gone, 'Right, I'll guarantee that, if my man can still be allowed to play for us, he won't get sent off, booked or even commit a foul.'

And they turned round and looked at him and they said, 'Mr Gardner, we do not run this league like the mafia.'

And that was the end of that. They gave me another fucking year's ban.

JOE JUNIOR

I am 16 now and know Bill through him being friends with my dad where we live in Surrey. Hardly anyone knows this hooligan stuff, because he didn't come and brag about the football. One of my mates had that ICF book, and I had it in my bag at work one day. And one of my mates walked past, looked and said, 'I know that bloke and it's Bill Gardner. He's been my football coach since I was about five.' And he went, 'Well, what's he doing on there?' Bill Gardner is on the cover of that book and this guy said, 'He used to stand on the sidelines and not swear or say a word.' He said, 'I've known him since I was five and not once did he get mouthy to the ref or to the other coaches. He was such a nice normal bloke and you wouldn't know. Funny man.'

There's two sides to Bill Gardner. I've seen him turn with Pauly and Stanford once when they were taking the piss because he loves animals. We would call him Dr Doolittle, and at the end of the night Stanford said, 'All right, Dr Doolittle.'

Gardner got that glazed look on his face, and Paul's gone, 'Oh, calm down, I'm only having a fucking laugh.'

But he fucking switched, and you think, Fucking hell, mate, you wouldn't want to be on the wrong side of that man.

GOOD AFTERNOON, GENTLEMEN, THE NAME'S BILL GARDNER

GLEN

I support Man United so I've got no West Ham stories of Bill as such, but I've known Bill for five years through youth football. I met Bill on a goalkeeper's course when on a trip to America. We stayed in a little place called Canton. It was a little village in upstate New York, and we stayed on some university campus along with about 15 boys between the ages of 12 and 16. Me, Bill and my cousin, Wayne, plus a few other dads, we took an overnight trip to Montreal, which was just across the border. It's a real kicking sort of town with plenty going on. But part of that trip included an open-top-bus tour around the streets of Montreal. Bill rolled up looking smart. He had his Burberry hat, leather jacket, Lonsdale bag, and all that.

So we were sitting on this open-top bus, with beautiful weather in this lovely city. Everyone was chatting away on this trip, which was a real bumpy ride. We turned around and Bill was fast asleep. He'd missed the whole lot. He didn't see one bit of it from the minute we got on until the minute we got off. And that was typical of Bill the whole trip. Anywhere you went, if you'd be sitting in a car with Bill, you'd be chatting away and you would look at him and think, Why isn't he answering me? and he'd be fast asleep. He was forever kipping. The minute he sat the cheeks of his arse down in a chair somewhere he'd fall asleep.

On that particular trip up to Canada we were in a four-wheel-drive people carrier. Bill was sat in the back, with me and my cousin in the front. We pulled up at the

Canadian border and Customs came over to us and they saw me, got my passport, and then they saw my cousin and looked at his passport. Then they said, 'Who's in the back?' and we said, 'Oh, our mate.' So they opened the back and they sort of jumped back. And they were shocked. The guy's exact words were, 'I've never seen a meaner-looking dude in my life.'

We went shopping in Montreal and the prices were dirt cheap because at the time you were getting three Canadian dollars for one pound but the price of the goods is the same. So a pair of trainers worth £60 would be £20. So Bill was like, 'I'm having some of that; I'm going shopping.' And when he came back, he's gone, 'I've bought myself a nice outfit to travel home in.'

So we've gone, 'All right, let's have a look.'

He said, 'I ain't going to show you. Just wait until you see it.'

The day to go home eventually came and we were waiting for Bill to come out of his room to see him with his new clobber on. And he walked out in this matching powder-blue towelling T-shirt and long shorts. He looked like a fucking teletubby. It looked like what you'd dress a two-year-old in. He thought he looked the bollocks, but everyone was like, nudge, nudge, wink, wink, you know, because no one can say anything to Bill.

The colour and the fact it was towelling like stuff back in the 1980s, and the long shorts that came down to the top of his big old calves – and he has funny legs – meant you couldn't miss him. He was like this big blob of powder blue. But we couldn't say anything because he thought he looked cool – and that's good enough for us. He's got some front.

Another thing I remember from that trip was when we had gone out driving one day and we saw this bar with a ladies' night on, so everyone's gone, 'We're having some of that.' My cousin Wayne was driving and they're really strict about speeding in America. So we were travelling through this town doing about 45 in a 30-speed zone. All of a sudden you heard sirens and the flashing lights have come on. So the Old Bill have pulled us over and these two state troopers have stepped out and have come round each side of the car – driver and passenger side. And it's a right overkill. They had two great big searchlights beamed in on us and they commanded us to wind down the window. Then they told us to turn off the engine and not to move. Don't step out of the car. Don't do anything. Where's your ID? Where's your driving licence? Well, we haven't got them. We don't carry driving licences; we're English.

Now bear in mind this is a year after September 11th and they are just paranoid in the States. And these two Old Bill are really on our case with me and my cousin. They're getting touchy and feeling their guns and all that. We couldn't explain who we were and we couldn't get it through to them that we don't carry ID. So at that stage Bill leaned forward and said, 'Here, mate, I've got a tattoo on me arm. Look, I'm Bill.'

And that cracked the ice. They cracked up laughing.

They could not stop laughing the pair of them, and with that they just looked at each other, shook their heads and said, 'Clear off, the lot of ya.' And that was it; we got away with it, basically because there ain't another one like Bill.

IAN

I first came across Bill in 1976 when I seriously started to go to football. Being a Spurs fan, Bill came across with a very big reputation in those days and obviously lived up to it. Over the next four years I had a few run-ins with Bill.

You would meet up with the boys at Tottenham and you'd ask, 'Where is everybody going today?'

And they'd go, 'We're away to so-and-so. We've got to watch out because West Ham's at home, so they will be about.'

Then you hear a name: Bill Gardner. And you think, What's this name? And as the years go by you realise this football thing was very frightening as a youngster, but it was an experience. In the 1970s and 1980s football terrace violence was everything to end with on a Saturday. It's not like now where you get football Monday to Sunday. Back then, Saturday aggro on the terraces was as common as fish and chips, and my team was Spurs because as a kid I wanted to watch Jimmy Greaves play.

So you would come across different people from different clubs. It was part and parcel of a Saturday afternoon, going and hanging around with the herberts, scarves around your wrists. You could wear your colours. You'd send out a little scouting party: Tottenham are coming, West Ham are coming. Who is this firm coming up the escalators? It was just everyone trying to hold their own little bit of ground. It was part and parcel of a Saturday afternoon and, if you weren't a part of that, it was pointless being there.

In 1980 I was asked to join a local football team – Woodhatch FC. My mate said, 'Come along and sign up, we're having a friendly.' So I went along, went in the changing rooms and got ready. I signed on, and the fellow went, 'Listen up, lads, this is our new manager, Bill Gardner.' I thought, I know that name, and I looked up and there he was, as large as life. I thought, Bloody hell, I hope he doesn't remember me. But it was a needless thought. Bill doesn't carry grudges for something like that, because in those days you had a fight with someone and, if you got in trouble, you got in trouble. It wasn't as if you had a running vendetta.

So I signed on with all the other guys: Wraithy, Gainy, Sullivan, Wilkins, Campsie, Hughes, Stanford, Procter, Pitman, Quinny, and I played right through until about 1990. Then I helped Bill run the side for a while. We had a very good side and it was like joining a family; it was close-knit and, if one player had a problem, everyone would try to help him. We did a lot with that team. Bill is very tactically minded and a very clever man and he put a lot of work into that side. To be honest, as a football manager, I think he could have gone a lot further in local football. Certainly semi-pro level. He had this ability to get you to believe in yourselves. He was dominant and a really strong motivator. He got us to play as a team. The confidence and belief he gave you would rub off on the whole team. He was very strong-minded and proud of what he was doing.

I've lived in Redhill all my life and everybody knew Bill worked on the door at the local nightclub. And again the reputation of Bill on the door was second to none. A lot of people you would meet would go, 'Yeah, we know Bill Gardner; we go down that nightclub; we go to football.' They don't know Bill Gardner. They don't know the side that I know or all the lads that play football at Woodhatch know: the hours he gives up for young kids for nothing, picking the balls up, taking them training, sorting the kit. At the end of the day he would be happy to see one of those kids go all the way, pro or semi-pro, and just know he'd helped that lad on the way.

And anyone that knows Bill knows he's not one for taking anything. He's been with Sarah for many, many years. He's a husband, a father to Danny and James, and he has spent hours travelling up and down the country taking them to football, watching them play football and trying to help them go pro. I can remember him going out of his way to help many a person. He is also generous and if I ever borrow anything from him he would just say, 'Give it back to me when you've got it, Ian.'

He is just different class. As a man he really is different gear. For him to go through his court troubles with the football, the leg breaks and the arthritis problems and still get up to go to work and do things, he is someone to be proud of. I think I can speak for everyone that's played for him and knows him that it is a pleasure and honour to play for Bill Gardner. I feel lucky that Bill Gardner is someone I can call my friend. I think back to when I looked up that day and heard 'this is Bill Gardner', and I thought, Oh my good God, of all the people to see. But it's been 25 years of true friendship and I would go anywhere to help that man, as he would me.

ANDY SWALLOW

For me Bill Gardner was West Ham in the late 1970s, until the ICF relieved him of his duties. It was refreshing to have a man who stood for West Ham, unlike the arrogant Mile End. I've been to many games with Bill in England and Europe and endured a lengthy court case standing alongside him as a co-defendant. Over the years there is so much that can be told and said of Bill. In truth, I wouldn't know where to begin, except to say for myself and many other West Ham fans we will always have the utmost respect for him as a fan and a man, and I wish him well with this book.

CHAPTER NINE

THANKS, GENTLEMEN, BUT I'LL HAVE THE LAST WORD

From the age of 18 I was widely marked up as the leader of the West Ham fans. I never knew why. I was just being me. I never organised trouble at football matches but, when it went off, something inside me seized the time to take control of dangerous situations. I can honestly say I never once felt frightened – I don't know why, I should have been, but I never was. And I only ever whacked people who wanted to whack me.

No one has ever really known the real me. Only my girlfriend and partner, Sarah. She's been my rock for 23 years. She has seen it all – my fight for my sanity and my fight for life – but I don't ever give up. Losing is a word that I don't understand. Even when I played football I was never the most gifted of players, but teams always wanted me to be in their side because I was a winner. I used to inspire the others around me. Five broken legs proved my commitment.

I never ever left a man down at a football match. How many of you in life have turned away, pretending not to see something like a woman being attacked or two drunks attacking one man in a street? And you've turned your head and pretended it wasn't happening, because it wasn't you. It's not my problem – that's the general attitude people have. I've never been like that. If I see anyone in trouble, it doesn't matter who they are, who they support or what colour or creed they are, I won't stand by and let people be bullied. I know what it is like to be bullied. I would never let that happen in my life as long as I've got breath in my body.

My life has been a roller-coaster ride, full of pain, both physically and mentally. I found strength in my family and the will to survive. When my first son was born, that was the end for me. I have been trying to put right the wrongs I might have done since then. But I would never change anything that previously I've done.

If being loyal to my friends and showing courage in adverse situations is wrong, then I am a guilty man. But the things I stand for are loyalty, courage and honour. They are values lost in society today. I can stand here and say there's not a person on this planet who could say I let them down – friend or foe – and not one of you would